365 ways to
meet people
in Cleveland

365 ways to
meet people
in Cleveland

Miriam Carey

GRAY & COMPANY, PUBLISHERS
CLEVELAND

Gray & Company, Publishers
1588 E. 40th Street
Cleveland, Ohio 44103
(216) 431-2665
www.grayco.com

ISBN 1-886228-45-0

Printed in the United States of America
10 9 8 7 6 5 4 3 2 1

Acknowledgments

When I was in school, I was never one to get involved, and I'll always regret that. It wasn't until I entered the working world that I understood the value of networking, volunteering, and broadening my horizons. I have to thank some of my favorite institutions for forcing me to get involved and stay involved. Through such organizations as the Press Club of Cleveland, the March of Dimes, the Cleveland Film Society, the First Friday Club, the Cleveland Film Festival, and the Playhouse Square Foundation, I've made friends, gained business contacts, and developed skills that I value very much. These groups—and the people that run them—came in quite handy while I was writing this book.

And through them, I've learned about still more groups. One of the most daring and productive is the Community Partnership for Arts and Culture, which is dedicated to bringing arts and cultural organizations together. Many thanks to Tom Schorgl for always sharing. The Ohio Arts Council, the Cleveland Convention and Visitors Bureau, University Circle Incorporated, and the many arts institutions in Cleveland all do an excellent job of providing information and developing programming that's worth writing about.

And, finally, there are all those friends and associates who contributed their thoughts, time, and effort to this book. I call them the Romance Task Force. They are: Anna Vedouras, Marcie Goodman, Sarah Crump, Denise Dufala, Ellen and Pete Kwiatkowski, Gavin Carey, Anthony Alessandrini, Billy Bass, Rich Osborne, Karen Schaefer, Brian Diehl, Bill Guentzler, Courtney Clarke, Candace Bowen, Ellen Stein-Burbach, Betsy O'Connell, M. Jane Christyson, Courtney Watson, Mary Gallagher, Jerry Fragapane, April Baer, Dave Pignanelli, Dan Morgan, Heather Price, Paula Coakely, Brian Baer, Donna Lee, Kevin Floyd, Patrick Shepheard, Kathleen Colan, and Diana Greenberg.

Thanks, always, to the crack staff at Gray and Company.

Introduction

Recently I wrote a book called 52 *Romantic Outings in Greater Cleveland*, a guide for Northeast Ohio couples. I was pleased to see lovers young and old show up for book signings, vowing to use the book as their personal guide to breaking the dinner-and-a-movie rut. I felt pretty good about myself—until the singletons started walking by. They'd pick up the book, look at me accusingly, and ask, "Romantic outings, huh? How 'bout finding me a date first?"

Though I don't think I can play matchmaker to the entire city, here's a start. Three hundred sixty-five ideas—places to go, events to attend, organizations to get involved with, and things to try (whether you're single or not) that will get you into the mix, shake up your social life, and force you to meet new people and try new things.

Just before I finished this book, I got an e-mail from a friend I'd met recently by getting involved in a new organization, reminding me, "nothing changes if nothing changes." This simple phrase encapsulates the purpose of 365 *Ways to Meet People in Cleveland*. Get off your chair, get into the community—drive to the other side of town! Do something today to change what your life will be like tomorrow.

Sometimes it takes just a nudge in the right direction to meet new friends, establish interesting business contacts, or search for true love. Use this book as a starting point and branch out from there. The opportunities in Cleveland will surprise and delight you at every turn.

I can't promise you'll get a date if you read this book. But I can guarantee that if you pursue just a few of these leads, you'll have ample opportunity to meet some fascinating new people.

Partner with the Playhouse

When it comes to attracting Cleveland's young, up-and-coming crowd of newly anointed professionals, **PLAYHOUSE SQUARE PARTNERS** leads all others. This highly active group raises funds for Playhouse Square and has fun doing it. Socialites will appreciate the group's frequent events; theater fans will like the special previews and other perks that come only with membership. Call Playhouse Square to find out how you can get involved; they'll connect you with a friendly, outgoing committee that you can contribute your talents to while forging new contacts.

Playhouse Square Partners, 1375 Euclid Ave., Cleveland, (216) 575-1781

GREAT OPENING LINE AT A FILM FESTIVAL:
"Which do you like better, the Cedar Lee or the Cinematheque?"

Get together to conserve public sculpture

You don't have to be a sculptor, architect, or 3-D designer to volunteer with the Sculpture Center's **Sculpture Conservation** Program, but you're likely to meet some folks who are. Once every year, the Sculpture Center chooses an outdoor public sculpture to spruce up. They hire conservators to lead the project, but always need volunteers to help. After the project is finished, stay involved with the center by attending their quarterly Sculptor's Forums where topics relating to the art of sculpture are discussed. Call to volunteer and find out the forum schedule.

The Sculpture Center, 1834 E. 123rd St., Cleveland, (216) 229-6527

Lead a kazoo band

Bring together your neighborhood by starting a **KAZOO BAND**. No kidding. Such bands provide some of the best entertainment at community and small-town parades. Being in a traditional kazoo band requires nothing more than a 50-cent kazoo available at most drugstores (in the kids' party section) or at Pat Catan's Craft Center locations throughout Greater Cleveland. Kazoos in hand, all you need is a willing group of men and women, and a repertoire of songs. Band members simply need to hum to make music. For best results, cull performers from neighborhood groups or the PTA—the neighborhood kids will get a kick out of seeing Mom and Dad in a parade. Keep it simple, and you'll soon know everyone in your neighborhood, and they'll know you. Don't forget to call your city hall to arrange a slot in the parade.

Pat Catan's Craft Centers, call (440) 786-7402 for a location near you

Share what you know

Here's a way to get paid for meeting new people: **TEACH**. Most communities in Northeast Ohio sponsor adult education classes, and they need instructors. If you're an accountant, teach a class on managing personal finances. If you're good with a glue gun, head a class on wreath making. Target your class to a group of people you'd like to hang out with, and see who shows up. You may discover a new talent, and maybe even acquire a following. So call your city's recreation board to find out how to get on the roster.

Play like a kid

Indulge your video game addiction without a bunch of high-scoring teenagers hanging around making you look bad. Adult gamers go to the **POWER PLAY GAME ROOM** because it brings out the kid in them while the liquor license keeps out the kids. Everyone is transformed into a kid upon entering, so it's okay—even encouraged—to walk up to a stranger and say, "Wanna play?" (Many of the games pit two or more players against each other.) Tue–Sat noon–2 a.m.

Power Play Game Room, 2000 Sycamore St., Cleveland, (216) 696-7664

Shop with the outdoorsy types

One way to meet outdoorsy types is to shop where they shop. **THE WILDERNESS SHOP** has stores on the east and west sides of town and carry everything you need to enjoy the outdoors. (They let you try stuff out, too.) Spend a little time browsing through the camping section of the store on a regular basis, and you'll likely encounter someone who likes camping as much as you do. Even better, through the employees and bulletin boards at the store, you can learn about organized outdoor activities taking place around town. The Wilderness Shops are open Mon 11 a.m.–9 p.m., Tue–Fri 10 a.m.–9 p.m., Sat 10 a.m.–6 p.m., and Sun noon–5 p.m.

The Wilderness Shop, 18636 Detroit Ave., Lakewood, (216) 521-9100;
1798 Coventry Rd., Cleveland Hts., (216) 321-4731

CLEVELAND FACT

There are more than 80 different ethnic groups living and thriving in Cleveland.

Cultivate your community

There are more than 190 **community gardens** in Cuyahoga County. One, at E. 35th Street and Cedar Avenue, was created by juvenile offenders in cooperation with the Ohio State University extension service, 4-H clubs, and many volunteers collectively known as the Green Team. Whether through big projects, like this one, or at simple neighborhood gardens, the hands-on labor of gardening brings people together. To volunteer at an existing garden or to start one in your own community, contact the Ohio State University Extension service. They'll point you in the right direction. From there, you can meet other gardeners, make a difference in the community, and develop a rewarding hobby.

Ohio State University Extension, 2490 Lee Blvd., Suite 108, Cleveland Hts., (216) 397-6000

Join the hunt

Antiquing can be a lonely hobby, but in June, antiquers gather to revel—together—in their love for antiques at the **LARCHMERE ANTIQUES FAIR**. Some of Northeast Ohio's best collectors are there, and crowds of antiquers move from booth to booth with an eye for detail and a desire to bargain. Call the Larchmere Antiques Fair for dates and times.

Larchmere Antiques Fair, at Larchmere Blvd. and E. 128th St., Cleveland, (216) 421-8394

Shop where the social shop

Become a regular at a local resale shop like the **APPLE CORR**, a consignment shop for upscale men's and women's clothing, where chatty bargain hunters and a very friendly and vocal staff love sharing tips with each other. You'll likely find a new shopping buddy here who will reveal names and locations of other great consignment stores in the area. The Apple Corr is open Mon–Sat 10 a.m.–6 p.m. with hours till 8 p.m. on Mon and Thu, and Sun noon–5 p.m.

Apple Corr, 19347 Detroit Rd., Rocky River, (440) 356-4747

Hang at the coffee shop

Explore your love of folk music and the beatnicky atmosphere of the **ARABICA COFFEEHOUSE** at University Circle. With its proximity to the major cultural institutions, hospitals, and educational venues in Cleveland, this coffeehouse almost guarantees you a seat next to an interesting person. The comfortable rooms welcome a diverse crowd of coffee sippers, and it's easy to start a chat with someone simply by asking, "What are you reading?" In the evenings, the house comes alive with folk music, poetry readings, and a mix of patrons that ranges from college students to surgeons. Sun–Tue 6:30 a.m.–11 p.m., Wed–Sat 6:30 a.m.–midnight.

Arabica at University Circle, 11300 Juniper Rd., Cleveland, (216) 791-0300

GREAT OPENING LINE AT A GIANT HOME IMPROVEMENT STORE:
"Do you know if Dunn Hardware sells lumber?"

Become an ambassador

Be a goodwill ambassador for by staffing a **TOURISM INFORMATION BOOTH**, at the airport, the Flats, or Tower City Center. Not only will you become an expert on where to go and what to do in town, but you'll meet a lot of people who need your help! The Convention and Visitors Bureau will train you, provide reference materials, and even pair you with another ambassador—so there's one new friend already. It's a fun job that keeps you on your toes and out in the community.

Convention and Visitors Bureau of Greater Cleveland, Tower City Center, Cleveland, (216) 875-6616

Attend some very social dinner parties

Every spring, the Lesbian/Gay Community Center hosts the **TADA! DINNER SERIES**, a fundraiser for the Center that features a variety of dinner parties at 35 individuals' homes that cost $35 to $100 per person, per party. The dinners, all with different themes, are very social, and the food is always sumptuous. Call the center in early February for a list of the parties being hosted this year, and sign up for as many dinners as you'd like.

Lesbian/Gay Community Center, 6600 Detroit Ave., Cleveland, (216) 651-5428

Spin with the indoor cyclists

Miss your bike when winter sets in? Join other cyclists who feel the withdrawal pangs at **STUDIO 82**, an indoor cycling facility where cyclists "spin" with groups on stationary bikes. During this intense aerobic workout, a group leader keeps you moving on high-tech stationary bikes through virtual terrain. Make a regular habit of these classes, and soon you'll be planning your first bike trip of the spring with new friends. Call to sign up for classes.

Studio 82, 13499 W. 130th St., North Royalton, (440) 582-4211

Learn ballroom dancing

If **DANCING THE TANGO** is on your "learn in this lifetime" list, be ready to fulfill at least one of your life's ambitions. Get together with a few friends or one partner and take a class at the Quirk Cultural Center. Instructors will teach you the basics, then you'll dance with classmates to work out your moves. Once you get good, invite some classmates to "tango night" at the Cleveland Ballroom Company (Sun 7 p.m.–8 p.m.). Classes are Thu from 7:30 p.m.–8:30 p.m.; call to sign up.

Quirk Cultural Center, 1201 Grant Ave., Cuyahoga Falls, (330) 971-8425
Cleveland Ballroom Company, 23500 Mercantile Rd., Beachwood, (216) 595-6955.

Social climbing

Rock climbing is a real buddy sport. Even if you've never tried it, you can take a rock-climbing class at the **Kendall Cliffs Rock Climbing Gym**, where staff members show you the ropes. Classes—from beginner to advanced—run throughout the day; just call to register. Once you know what you're doing, you can stop in anytime to practice scaling the walls. Make it your ultimate goal to climb this indoor facility's 35-foot-high arch, which spans the building. Friday night is ladies' night (half-price for female climbers)—a good night to be a man at the gym. Mon–Fri noon–10 p.m., Sat 10 a.m.–9 p.m., and Sun noon–8 p.m.

Kendall Cliffs Rock Climbing Gym, 6000 Kendall Park Rd., Peninsula, (330) 655-5489

Join these lunatics

Join the monthly **FULL MOON HIKE** in the Cuyahoga Valley National Park. You'll meet other hikers who enjoy the romance of bright night sky and an invigorating walk. December's darkened skies bring forth the longest night of the year, but the hike, which is suitable for beginners, goes every month. Call ahead to find out exactly where and when the group will meet and then just show up.

Full Moon Hike: The Long Night's Moon, Cuyahoga Valley National Park, various locations, (330) 650-4636

Take a riding class

If you love horses—or just want to try something new, take a **HORSEBACK-RIDING CLASS** at the MetroParks stable facilities in Brecksville. Classes of about 10 start up about every 6 weeks and cost less than $200. Beginners often continue on into intermediate classes. Once you get really good and get to know your classmates, schedule a day of riding together or plan an outing to a new riding facility. It's a very social sport. Call to check the schedule and sign up for class.

Cleveland MetroParks Brecksville Stables, 11921 Parkview Dr., Brecksville, (440) 526-6767

Learn a foreign language

Does the idea of a trip to Paris appeal to the romantic in you? Does dinner at a local Italian joint make you yearn for a trip to Rome? You might meet your counterpart at a **FOREIGN-LANGUAGE CLASS** while learning a new tongue. At the Berlitz Language Center, instructors can teach you just about any language—and quickly. Tailored for businesspeople who need or want to enhance their skills, this school is located right downtown. Not only will you meet people in Cleveland, you'll have a better chance of meeting someone in Rome—once you learn to speak as they do. Call for a schedule and to register for class.

Berlitz Language Center, 1300 E. 9th St., Cleveland, (216) 861-0950

TIPS AND REMINDERS

When you're volunteering for an organization, be bold and ask them for the most social assignments—they'll usually be glad to accommodate you if you tell them what you're up to.

Try sand volleyball

Want to meet active and sporting types? Every summer, the Cleveland Sport and Social Club organizes summer **SAND VOLLEYBALL LEAGUES** and tournaments. You don't have to be a member, but there is a small fee for participating in the league. Register as an individual and they'll put you on a team, or you can build your own team. Play a game or three of volleyball on the sandy courts at Whiskey Island in the Flats, then spend some time socializing with your teammates. Call for a game schedule and to register.

Cleveland Sport and Social Club, 1322 Old River Rd., Cleveland, (216) 696-3770 (games at Whiskey Island)

Chat at Nighttown's circular bar

Nighttown feels like **A PROPER IRISH PUB**, and when there's music playing, or a local author touting his book, this restaurant with its cozy bar attracts a chummy crowd of regulars. The circular bar lets voices carry across the room, and patrons get involved in one another's conversations. Mon–Sat 11:30 a.m.–midnight and Sun 10 a.m.–midnight.

Nighttown, 12387 Cedar Rd., Cleveland Hts., (216) 795-5050

Make friends on the Fourth

Even if you're the most dedicated Anthrax fan, you'll have to admit that hearing one of the world's best orchestras play a free **Independence Day concert** on Public Square each year is something special. Arrive downtown early to claim a spot for your lawn chair, bring a cooler filled with non-alcoholic beverages and a few snacks, then mix, mingle, and get to know your neighbors. The music created by the orchestra bring peace and tranquility to the busiest part of downtown, the light show that accompanies the concert brings excitement to the square, and the combination puts everyone in a sociable mood. The concert time varies from year to year, so call for a schedule.

The Cleveland Orchestra, (216) 231-7300 (annual 4th of July concert held at Public Square, downtown Cleveland)

Plug in to the rock scene

Music fans who want to be with the in-crowd at the Rock and Roll Hall of Fame and Museum join **PLUGGED IN**, the hall's official affiliate membership group. It puts on fun parties and programs that bring music luminaries like Muddy Waters to town and also brings Clevelanders together. Pick a committee and get involved. Most groups meet monthly to plan their next party or program. Call to find out when and where the next meeting will be.

Plugged In/Rock and Roll Hall of Fame and Museum, 1 Key Plaza, Cleveland, (216) 781-7625

Ski with a cutting edge club

Since 1978, the Esprit **SKI & SPORTS CLUB** has kept "on the cutting edge of ski-ing." They describe themselves as fun-loving African Americans who love this win-ter sport. But they also host summer activities including an annual racquetball party in the spring, Splash Party in the summer, and ongoing activities in cycling, golfing, skating, camping, and whitewater rafting. They ask that you get member-ship and event information through the mail or from their website.

Esprit Ski & Sports Club, Inc., P.O. Box 94151, Cleveland, 44101-4151, www.nbs.org/clubs/esprit/info.html

Fish off the city's busiest pier

Grab a line and a pole and head to **EDGEWATER PARK PIER**. Don't have a line and a pole? Stop at Ketchmore Rod & Tackle on your way. Just a few blocks away from Edgewater, Ketchmore has all the bait and tackle you'll need, and fishing poles starting at $20. Though Edgewater may not have the greatest fishing in the world, it's a very busy pier in the summer with plenty of people to talk to. This jaunt is especially fun and sociable if you bring along the kids to teach them the basics. Pretty soon, you'll be fishing and chatting with the locals who come here regularly to bag some Lake Erie perch. The crowd is friendly, and if you've got the time, you might even get a nibble on your line. The pier is open from dusk until dawn.

Edgewater Park Pier, Edgewater Park, 3600 John Nagy Blvd., Cleveland, (216) 881-8141
Ketchmore Rod & Tackle, 5405 Detroit Ave., Cleveland, (216) 961-1770

TIPS AND REMINDERS

Ignore your mother's advice. Talk to strangers.

Invest in a networking opportunity

Get in touch with the **INVESTING COMMUNITY** by joining the Cleveland Chapter of the American Association of Individual Investors. They offer eight city wide, open-to-the-public meetings every year. Attendance varies by topic, but often 100 or more people participate. At a typical meeting you'll hear a financial professional discuss investment concepts and have the opportunity to ask questions and participate in the discussion. Call for information about meetings and membership.

American Association of Individual Investors, Cleveland Chapter, (440) 884-9063

Hunt for hubcaps

Here's an excellent place to bump into car buffs. If they're at **MARILYN'S HUBCAP HEAVEN**, they care about their wheels. This unusual store carries just about every kind of hubcap you can imagine, and people mill about here on Saturday afternoons with a mission to find just the right one. Mix with the crowd and ask questions of other customers. Next thing you know, you'll be debating the merits of whitewalls, and lamenting the loss of the winter tire to the all-season radial.

Marilyn's Hubcap Heaven, 13840 Puritas Ave., Cleveland, (216) 252-1994

Discover world music

Check out one of the concerts sponsored by the Kent State University **School of World Music**. Most weeks during the academic year the school hosts a world music lecture or concert. This series fits right in with the vibrant music scene at Kent, and the informal university atmosphere makes it easy to have impromptu discussions and get to know the musicians and attendees. Call the school, or check its website (www.ksu.edu) for schedules and ticket information. Most concerts don't require advance tickets, so it's easy to attend on a whim.

Center for World Music at KSU, Kent State University Campus, Kent, (330) 672- 3871

Tri dancing

If you decide to take a dance class at Tri-C, your biggest problem will be deciding which one. **DANCE CLASSES** from ballet to tap keep you in shape, and all the activity on campus will throw you in the mix with plenty of other self-motivated types who want to keep learning. Encourage friends to come with you, or attend alone. Make new friends by attending recitals with fellow students, or set a date to go out dancing together. Call for a schedule of classes, there's a new series every semester.

Cuyahoga Community College, Metro Campus, 2900 Community College Ave., Cleveland, (216) 987-4103
Cuyahoga Community College, East Campus, 4250 Richmond Rd., Beachwood, (216) 987-2000
Cuyahoga Community College, West Campus, 1100 W. Pleasant Valley Rd., Parma, (216) 987-5000

Lure a friendly fisher

Join the West Cleveland **WALLEYE ASSOCIATION**. Show up at one of their monthly meetings to learn everything about Walleye—where to find 'em, how to lure 'em, and the best way to cook 'em. You'll soon be lured into the club's expeditions, with an inside scoop on the best spots and some new fishing buddies. They meet on the second Thursday of each month at 7:30 p.m.

West Cleveland Walleye Association, 20300 Hilliard Rd., Rocky River, (440) 835-2892

Take a photography class

If you like photography, nature outdoor photography, then get involved in the Cleveland MetroParks PHOTOGRAPHY CLUB. Shutterbugs meet at MetroParks nature centers with cameras in hand to learn from experts about how and when to photograph the outdoors. Classmates meet in small groups to share and critique pictures and plan their next outing. Call to find out when and where the next meeting is and get on the mailing list.

Cleveland MetroParks Photography Club, (216) 351-6300

The best new-moms network

"The first thing I did after I had a baby was get involved with my local **early childhood PTA**," says Jennifer Stoffel, author of the book *Cleveland Family Fun*. "It's a great word-of-mouth network for new moms." A bit misnamed, these groups don't involve teachers—just parents. Moms, mostly, get together for outings, meetings, and parties for the kids. They swap information about kid-friendly activities, babysitters—they even trade or sell hand-me-downs, like strollers and toys. Not all communities have early childhood PTA groups, and some are stronger than others (Lakewood has one of the largest). Call your local school board to find out if there's one in your community.

Go where the swing dancers go

Here, you can find out *everything* that has to do with **SWING DANCING** in Cleveland. This website tells where to take lessons and where to dance once you know what you're doing. It is the clearinghouse for Cleveland swing dancers, who contribute regularly to the site by adding to the events listings and providing quick tips on what to expect at each dance club or event. Whether you're 16 or 62, you'll find a spot that's right for you.

Cleveland Swings, www.clevelandswings.com

New friendship is in the stars

Do you while away the evening hours gazing at the sky in wonderment? Learn what happens up there. The Chagrin Valley **ASTRONOMICAL SOCIETY**, founded in 1963, holds monthly meetings and astronomy discussions. They also offer regular conventions and "star parties" year-round as opportunities for socializing and stargazing. Write or check their website for a schedule and membership information. On the West Side, check into the Cuyahoga Astronomical Association.

Chagrin Valley Astronomical Society, P.O. Box 11, Chagrin Falls, 44022, www.en.com/users/lp/#Overview
Cuyahoga Astronomical Assn., P.O. Box 868, North Olmsted, 44070, www.en.com/users/cygnus/caadoc.htm

Learn to kayak

Try out a kayak—in the middle of a sporting goods store! You can at Newman Outfitters, where an indoor pool lets KAYAKERS try out each model. Classes are held here frequently, so you can learn the basics when you buy your kayak. Stop in for an evening paddle, sign up for a class, and get on the mailing list to find out when the next Newman-sponsored kayaking trip will be. Store is open Mon–Fri 10 a.m.–9 p.m., Sat. 10 a.m.–7 p.m.

Newman Outfitters, 6025 Kruse Dr., Solon, (440) 248-7000

Meet Tremont's trendy

If you're hip, trendy, on the scene, and have a little money to spend, walk the **TREMONT ART WALK**. On the second Friday of every month, the galleries and shops of Tremont stay open late for art lovers and pub crawlers who enjoy sampling the cutting edge of urban art in Cleveland. The streets come alive with pedestrians, who trade quick critiques with friends they pass in the street. After touring the galleries, art-walkers tour the pubs and get to know each other. The art walk runs from about 7 p.m. to 2:30 a.m.

Tremont West Development Corporation, 2190 Professor Ave. #2, Cleveland, (216) 575-0920

A garlic-lovers' get-together

If you love garlic—I mean, really *love* the stuff—go meet other **GARLIC JUNKIES** at Medina's Garlic Festival in September. With live music and entertainment, and the seductive smell of garlic permeating the air, you'll be in garlic heaven for a day. You won't be able to resist the roasted garlic, garlic desserts, or garlic-buttered bread, so bring breath mints if you're going to flirt. Call for festival dates.

Garlic Festival, Barco's Liberty Gardens, 935 West Liberty Street, Medina, (330) 722-3038

Golf . . . at night!

Golf takes on a much more social atmosphere **in the dark**. During the summer months, the Cleveland MetroParks golf courses—there are six courses in the system—occasionally stay open after sunset and provide golfers with glow-in-the-dark balls. On one of these evenings you'll encounter lots of other golfers searching for lost balls and trying to find their way around the darkened links. "You can blame the darkness for bad shots, and you never know who or what you will find in the rough searching for your golf ball," says Jane Christyson, marketing director for the parks. "Over the years it's turned into a great singles event."

Cleveland MetroParks Golf Ranges, various locations, (440) 232-7247

Go for a chili dog

Here's a recommendation from WCPN's morning anchor, April Baer: "In the wee hours of the morning, the best places to visit are the **HOT DOG STANDS** on Lorain Avenue. I find the dogs and conversation are the best at Old Fashion Hot Dogs, where the menu selection may be limited, but it's the real thing—very down home and friendly. Trust me on this one: walk in, ask for two with chili, cheese, and onion, and a side of fries, and smile nicely at the person on the stool next to you. The stories will just start to flow." Open 24/7.

Old Fashion Hot Dogs, 4008 Lorain Ave., Cleveland, (216) 432-3700

TIPS AND REMINDERS

Put the word out. People who are already couples are always interested in making couples of other people. Let them live vicariously through you by setting you up on dates every once in a while.

Advertise

Even if you said you would never place a **PERSONAL AD**, try it just once. Make it more fun by recruiting a friend to place an ad at the same time you do; then compare notes with each other—hey, you might even wind up trading dates. For best results, place your ads in a local publication that you think your ideal date would read (*Scene* magazine if you're into rock and roll, the *Free Times* if you lean leftward politically, and *Cleveland Magazine* if you're targeting the sophisticated crowd). If you decide to meet a few of the respondents, pick casual dates—coffee or a quick lunch—that you can build on if you like the person. Though you may be embarrassed about trying this out, many have had great success. There must be something to it.

Scene *Magazine*, *1375 Euclid Ave., Cleveland, (216) 241-7550*
***The* Free Times,** *1846 Coventry Rd., Cleveland Hts., (216) 321-2300*
Cleveland Magazine, *1422 Euclid Ave., Cleveland, (216) 771-2833*

Be a little bit country

If **LINE DANCING** appeals to the inner square dancer in you, learn all the best moves at the Boot Scoot'n Saloon. Regulars will teach you the steps, and once you catch on, it's fun to dance the night away. By the end of the evening, you might just know at least half the crowd by name. The most popular nights are Wednesday, Friday, and Saturday. Open 7 p.m.–2 a.m.

Boot Scoot'n Saloon, 4193 State Rd., Akron, (330) 939-7123

Craft a new friendship

Get into **ARTS AND CRAFTS** at Baycrafters, where professionals and art enthusiasts run classes and activities year round. If just being around other creative types is enough to stimulate you, sign up to help with a social event. Call to volunteer or sign up for a class—make sure you look through the catalog so you know if there's anything extra you'll need to bring along.

Baycrafters, off Porter Rd. in the Huntington Reservation of the Cleveland MetroParks, Bay Village, (440) 871-6543

Shop with the fresh food fanatics

If you're fanatical about fresh food, check out the **LAKEWOOD FARM MARKET**, which runs Wednesday afternoons from noon until 4 p.m. in the summer. Pick up farm-fresh produce from local producers and mingle with a cross-section of Lakewood's diverse population—young singles, fresh-food fans, and the active over-50 crowd converge here. The real food fans show up first thing to get their hands on the very freshest produce. That's when you should be there, too.

Lakewood Farm Market, at Detroit and Arthur Rds., Lakewood

Come back every week with the boomerang bunch

Not rain, nor snow, nor sleet can stop the **BOOMERANGS** from returning to Wade Park. Every Sunday from around 11 a.m. until 1 or 2 p.m., Cleveland Boomerang School is in session. Show up with or without a boomerang—instructors will help you make one—and show you how to throw it. It's a casual, drop-by-if-you-feel-like-it crowd. It's fun, it's free, and it's something you can always fall back on.

Cleveland Boomerang School, Wade Park, University Circle, (216) 289-6324

Roll out the barrel

One lonely hearts' delight on Friday nights is Podboy's. This **polka bar** turns into one hot dance party. It's not as traditional a polka night as some in Cleveland; the bands go for a more modern sound. But Podboy's is always packed with a fascinating mix of active older types who are serious about dancing. (Proprietor Michael Podboy is himself a find.) Single women can't stand alone in this bar for 10 minutes without getting swept up by some rakish and enthusiastic polka fiend. It gets a bit loud for conversation, but as far as meeting people, this one's a lock.

Podboy's, 20670 Lakeland Blvd., Cleveland, (216) 481-6453

Brown bag with the book club

You've got a standing lunch date with the literary set on the first Wednesday of every month. Bring your lunch to the Cleveland Public Library and join in the lively **BOOK DISCUSSION**. Stop by the Popular Library to pick up a brochure of the upcoming book selections (or call and they'll tell you), then just show up. If you don't like the books they're discussing, you could always start your own book club.

Cleveland Public Library Book Discussion Group, Louis Stokes Wing, Room 218, Cleveland, (216) 623-2800

Bowl in the grass

If you've grown a bit too . . . mature . . . for full-contact athletics but still want some exercise, fun, and outdoor time, join the Forest Hill **LAWN BOWLING** Club. Nothing adds class to bowling like doing it outdoors; you can wear better shoes— cleats if you like—and soak in the sunshine. Call ahead to see if the club can pair you with other players and to confirm the meeting time. Or stop by just to watch first. The club meets from the first week in May through the last week in September on Wed and Sat at 10 a.m. and Sun at 2 p.m.

Forest Hill Lawn Bowling Club, Forest Hill Blvd. at Terrace Rd., East Cleveland, (440) 449-5058

The night for adult ice-skating

You're never too old to go skating. And it is a great way to bump into people (literally) whom you otherwise wouldn't meet. **ADULT SKATE NIGHTS** at Winterhurst Ice Rink in Lakewood draw a crowd of skaters age 21 and over who are there for fun and socializing. The rink takes on a much calmer atmosphere than you'll remember from high school. Adult skate is on Mon and Thu nights from 8:30 to 11 p.m.

Winterhurst Ice Rink, 14740 Lakewood Hts. Blvd., Lakewood, (216) 529-4400

Stretch your horizons with the spiritual set

Open your mind with classes on yoga, healthy diet, and meditation and you'll also open your social life to new friends who aspire to enrich their lives. Bhumi's provides an opportunity for those interested in **SPIRITUAL EXPLORATION** through alternative living to meet and learn together. Class offerings vary, with yoga classes available almost all the time; call for a schedule and to sign up.

Bhumi's Yoga and Wellness Center, King James Plaza, 25068 Center Ridge Rd., Westlake, (440) 899-9569

A must-do for opera fans

Are you an opera fan looking for someone with whom you can attend performances? Check into the **OPERA PROGRAM** at the Cleveland Institute of Music. Every February, the Institute holds a class on opera that piques the interest of opera lovers and brings them together. The program focuses on a specific topic, providing an evening filled with beautiful music as well as information. But it's also an opportunity to socialize and make new friends for next season. Call for the schedule and to sign up.

Cleveland Institute of Music, 11021 East Blvd., Cleveland, (216) 791-5000

GREAT OPENING LINE AT A MALL FOOD COURT:
"Do you think we'd be better off at Chuck's Diner?"

Paddle as a team

Make friends with other families when you paddle a 34-foot voyager **canoe** at Hinckley Reservation. The canoes hold a dozen or so people, so invite along a family that you don't know too well yet—by the end of the trip you'll probably be the best of friends. MetroParks marketing director Jane Christyson promises that you'll "sing songs, hear stories, and sample the horrid dried meat that passed for food during the Great Lakes fur-trading era while costumed historical interpreters lead these trips that take you downstream toward history." The canoe trips are offered May through September; call to sign up for a trip.

Cleveland MetroParks Hinckley Reservation, of Bellus and State Rds., Hinckley, (216) 351-6300

Where die-hard sledders get extreme

Put the kids in the car and head to the **TOBOGGAN CHUTES** in Strongsville. You'll find a lot of other parents there doing the same thing. Refrigerated ice chutes guarantee that your day of tobogganing won't be slowed down by slush. They provide the toboggan; all you need is enough true grit to push yourself off the top of the chute. The chute is open Thu 6 p.m.–10 p.m., Fri 6 p.m.–10:30 p.m., Sat noon–10:30 p.m., and Sun noon–8 p.m.; call for holiday hours.

Chalet Recreation Area, Mill Stream Run Reservation, 16200 Valley Parkway, Strongsville, (440) 572-9990

Go to a small-town market

The **FARMER'S MARKET** held in downtown Oberlin on Saturday mornings in the summer brings together farmers, foodies, and college types for a morning filled with good food and plenty of opportunities to meet and greet. Strolling through bucolic Oberlin will put you in a friendly frame of mind while you shop—don't be surprised if you feel compelled to say "hello" to everyone you meet. The market is held on Saturdays, June through September from 8:30 a.m. to 2 p.m.

Oberlin farmer's market, Main Street, Downtown Oberlin (440) 775-1531

Get on a volleyball team

When summer comes around, get ready for Singles Sand Volleyball in Wickliffe. Sand **VOLLEYBALL TOURNAMENTS** get competitive here—but a great crowd shows up to bump and spike the ball. Contact the group early in the season to get on a team or create one of your own, or just show up some evening and they'll put you on a team. The games are held on Wednesdays at 7:30 p.m.

Singles Sand Volleyball, (216) 556-3662 (games held next to Borromeo Seminary, 28700 Euclid Ave., Wickliffe)

Cook something up

Cooking with strangers is a bonding experience. Try a class at the Loretta Paganini **COOKING SCHOOL**. Bring nothing with you but a good attitude and a hearty appetite; you'll eat what you cook at this class. The evening-long classes afford plenty of social time. Some are developed for couples; others are just for single people. Classes are offered year-round. Call for a catalog.

Loretta Paganini School of Cooking, 8613 Mayfield Rd., Hudson, (330) 835-3632

Perform

Got 10 minutes' worth of material? Try it out at **OPEN MIKE NIGHT** at Spill the Beans. Other aspiring musicians and comics will be there, and a friendly camaraderie develops. Stage fright? It's just as much fun to be a patron. The alcohol-free atmosphere is a welcome departure from the bar scene, and as each new act takes the stage, coffee drinkers share critiques on performances. Open mike night is usually Monday, when Spill the Beans closes at 10 p.m. Call to confirm that it's on the schedule.

Spill the Beans, 27940 Chardon Rd., Wickliffe, (440) 944-6560

Join a tennis club

The River Oaks Racquet Club is hopping year-round with **TENNIS** games and tournaments, so it's a great spot for tennis players looking for partners. Though River Oaks is a club that requires membership fees, the social opportunities make it worth the price. Open Mon–Thu 6 a.m.–11 p.m., Fri–Sat. 6 a.m.–10 p.m., Sun 8 a.m.–6 p.m.

River Oaks Racquet Club, 21220 Center Ridge Rd., Rocky River, (440) 331-4980

Hang at the Honey Hut

For years, the **HONEY HUT** has attracted a crowd of ice-cream fiends on warm summer nights. It's worth a trip there to be a part of the ice-cream social at the picnic tables just beyond the order window, and the chill of sweet ice cream spurs warm, spontaneous conversations. Open in the summer on Tue– Sat 11 a.m.–11 p.m., Sun noon–10 p.m.

Honey Hut Ice Cream, 6250 State Rd., Cleveland, (440) 885-5055

The center of the Lesbian/Gay community

If you're feeling alone in the Cleveland gay community, then stop in at the **LESBIAN/GAY COMMUNITY CENTER** as soon as possible to check out their busy schedule of support group meetings and social events. Sign up to help with fundraising activities, which will put you in touch with a host of people and events. Open Mon–Fri noon–10 p.m., and Sun 6:30 p.m.–9 p.m.

Lesbian/Gay Community Center, 6600 Detroit Ave., Cleveland, (216) 651-5428

Practice your softball swing

Love baseball? Need stress relief? Join the folks who converge on **SOFTBALL WORLD**. Rent a batting cage for a half-hour and hit a ball with friends or just blow off some steam by yourself. There are lots of others there working on their swings, and they all end up at the soda stand after a session. This is also a great place to get hooked up with a team or league—check the bulletin board in the rental house. Open daily 9 a.m.–5 p.m.

Softball World, 5500 West 130th St., Lakewood, (216) 362-8200

If you play your cards right . . .

Looking for a Bridge partner? There are plenty available at your local **BRIDGE CLUB**. Why not try the Monthly Whist Club in Broadview Heights? They play every Wednesday night at 7:30. Call for information and to get paired with a partner. If you don't know how to play, don't be left out—call (330) 722-8214 to find out where you can learn the game. For additional local clubs, call (330) 722-8214.

Monthly Whist Bridge Club, (440) 248-3983 (games at St. Michael's Woodside, 6025 East Mills Rd., Broadview Hts.)

Trek to the sci-fi film fest

The academic year brings with it another season of weekend films at the **CWRU FILM SOCIETY**. But the don't-miss event of the year is the society's Science Fiction Film Festival. Case Western Reserve University, a campus with a reputation for attracting geeks, comes alive for the SciFi Fest. If you want to meet a future engineer or a partner to travel to Star Trek conventions with, this is the place. Call the society early in the fall to get a schedule sent to you, and block out dates on your calendar for the SciFi Fest and other films you want to see.

Case Western Reserve University Film Society, Strosacker Auditorium, CWRU Campus, Cleveland, (216) 368-2354

TIPS AND REMINDERS

Try something new—and slightly terrifying—at least once a month. Soon, you'll discover that all the fun you've been missing isn't so terrifying after all.

Think globally, act locally—meet locals

Getting involved with **CITIZEN ACTION** will keep you involved with national issues on a local level. You'll distribute flyers, attend rallies, and coordinate local campaigns. Contact the Cleveland office, and they'll match your talent with an appropriate volunteer job, train you to do it, and keep your time commitment in mind. Tell them you're interested in working with groups of singles like yourself, and they'll be delighted to oblige—the more helping hands the better.

Citizen Action, 614 W. Superior Ave., Cleveland, (216) 861-5200

Become a leader in the Jewish community

Meet active young members of the Cleveland's **JEWISH COMMUNITY** at the Young Leadership Division of the Jewish Community Federation. This extremely active group hosts social, educational, and volunteer programs throughout the year that are targeted to members of the Jewish community aged 21 to 37. Become really active and you might find yourself attending a regional conference on behalf of the organization. Call to volunteer or find out about the next event.

Jewish Community Federation, 1750 Euclid Ave., Cleveland, (216) 566-9200

Network at work—you never know what might happen . . .

They say you should keep your work relationships all business, but once in awhile, you have let **friendships really blossom**. Take Mark Leddy and Cindy Barber, for example, "We'd known each other for a while," Mark says, "I was booking at Pat's in the Flats and I called Cindy all the time, because she was editor of the *Free Times*. She talked me into getting involved at the Beachland Ballroom, which she was starting up at the time, so I got involved in the project. It developed into something more. Now we own the Ballroom together."

An outdoor market offering tarot card readings

Be a part of the eclectic crowd that shows up each Saturday at **OPEN AIR AT MARKET SQUARE**. Musicians, artists, peddlers, and psychics congregate here to cater to a roving crowd. Stop and have your tarot cards read, or chat with the artists about their wares. With the live music and activities, you could easily spend an entire Saturday here meeting and talking with people and never be bored. Open Air at Market Square runs June though September on Sat 8:30 a.m.–4 p.m.

Open Air at Market Square/Ohio City Near West Development Corp., 2525 Market Ave., Cleveland, (216) 781-3222

Where the frog-lovers frolic

Want to meet some nice folks who will love you, warts and all? You'll find them at the Valley City **FROG JUMPING CONTEST** in August. First, learn how frog jumping is done at www.valleycity.org. And once you've found and trained a frog, try him out at the contest. Of course, if you don't have a frog, it's still a fun, sociable event to attend. The contest takes place every year.

Valley City Frog Jumping Contest, the Lazy T. Ranch, on Grafton Road between SR 252 (Columbia Road) and Marks Road, Valley City, (330) 483-1111

Shoot hoops

Looking for a pick-up game of **BASKETBALL** after work? Just listen for the sound of dribbling that starts up after 5:30 p.m. on weekdays at Lakewood Park and continues until dusk. It's informal—there are no leagues here—and easy to get in on a game. With plenty of people around, you'll have an audience. Become a regular, and you'll always have a friend to shoot hoops with. The courts are located near the tennis courts and next to the softball field on Lake Avenue west of Belle.

Lakewood Park, at Belle and Lake Ave., Lakewood, (call Lakewood City Hall for information (216) 521-7580)

Learn art at the ultimate art institution

CREATE ART and make some new friends at a class at the Cleveland Museum of Art. Throughout the year, special classes are offered for adult beginners and intermediates who want to study in Cleveland's most artistic setting. After class, grab a cup of coffee with your classmates at the museum cafe and discuss art in the sculpture garden. Call to sign up ahead of time for courses, and ask if you need to bring anything to class.

Cleveland Museum of Art, 11150 East Blvd., Cleveland, (216) 421-7340 x 461

Be a regular at this corner record store

Do you crave the intimacy of a **corner record store** where they know you by name? Become a regular at Record Revolution on Coventry—even if it's not in your neighborhood. Hang out in your favorite section, and strike up conversations with the staff. They'll point you to the right recordings, and if you stick around long enough, they also might point you to fans of the same music. But the real deal is the bargain CDs you'll find here—used CDs sometimes cost as little as 50 cents. Mon–Fri 11 a.m.–8 p.m., Sat 11 a.m.–9 p.m., and Sun noon–7 p.m.

Record Revolution, 1828 Coventry Rd., Cleveland Hts., (216) 321-7661

Dawdle with dog lovers

Do you live by the saying, "Love me, love my dog"?
Then come to the UNOFFICIAL DOG PARK of
the West Side—Rocky River's Elmwood Park.
On Saturday mornings from about 8:30 until 3
in the afternoon, pets and their owners converge on
the park to frolic in the great outdoors.
Bring a tennis ball or a Frisbee, and talk with
the other humans while Rover has his day.

Elmwood Park Dog Walking, Rocky River (call Rocky River Recreation Dept. (440) 356-5657)

The popular spot for a morning dip

Are you a water baby? The best place to meet other **swimmers** is at the LifeStart fitness club downtown, where a heated, Olympic-size pool lets swimmers share lanes through every season. You do have to be a member to come here, but the cost is worth it if you work downtown and love to swim. The early-morning crowd is the most active and just about all of them are downtown professionals. Don't be afraid to don a pair of flippers or water resisters available in the pool area—it won't harm your reputation as a hard-nosed lawyer to be seen looking like Aqua Man, and it might be a great conversation starter. Open Mon–Sat 5:30 a.m.–9 p.m., closed Sun.

LifeStart Athletic Club, 1375 E. 9th St., Cleveland, (216) 621-0770

Help bring the theater to at-risk kids

CLEVELAND PUBLIC THEATRE, an excellent place to see a play, is also a great place to make a difference. At-risk kids have an opportunity here to learn about the theater by working with volunteers—could be you—who teach them how to put on a show while they learn about art, business, and friendship. Even if you're not an actor, the theatre needs volunteers to do everything from serving lunch, to constructing sets, to making sure the kids have what they need to put on a great performance. Call to sign up as a volunteer.

Cleveland Public Theatre, 6415 Detroit Ave., Cleveland, (216) 631-2727

Bust a rhyme

Got a poem in your head that's just busting to get out? Get thee to a **POETRY READING**! The Poets' League of Greater Cleveland sends out a monthly newsletter that lists a different poetry event or activity to participate in almost every day of the month. Whether it's a poetry reading at a coffee shop or a writer's workshop, you'll find at least one new thing to do every few weeks on this list—and you'll start networking with other poets like yourself. Call to get on the mailing list.

Poets' & Writers' League of Greater Cleveland, 2304 N. St. James Parkway, Cleveland Hts., (216) 932-8444

Take a special morning walk

Is your morning walk getting lonely? Try the **CHICKADEE WALK** in Mayfield Village. Here, groups meet to take a walk through the woods where the chickadees feed. Bring nothing but a sunny attitude with you on these winter hikes that are led by a chickadee aficionado. While you walk with the group, your resident expert tells you all about these tame little birds. And a group of folks who like a morning hike might just make this trail a regular meeting place, even after the chickadees are gone. Call to find out where and when to meet.

A. B. Williams Memorial Woods, Buttermilk Falls Pkwy., North Chagrin Reservation, Mayfield Village, (440) 473-3370

CLEVELAND FACT

According to a recent survey there are 60 single men for every 100 single women in the Cleveland Metropolitan area.

March into madness

BASKETBALL FANS are out in droves during March Madness—when college basketball rules, and fans survive on chicken wings and beer. You'll find a lot of them at the Winking Lizard downtown. With TVs lining the bar and good chicken wings available, this place becomes a home away from home for hoop fans during the season. Open Mon–Thu 11 a.m.–midnight, Fri–Sat 11 a.m.–2 a.m., Sun 11 a.m.–1 a.m.

Winking Lizard, 811 Huron Rd., Cleveland, (216) 589-0313

Aficionados love the huge wine list

A great place to see and be seen on a weekend night is **D'VINE WINE BAR**, with its large rooms, gigantic wine list, and delicious appetizers. Many patrons are here because they're into wine—making conversation easy amongst wine aficionados—and it's hard not to get caught up in debating the merits of this year's rainfall in Sonoma County. Sun–Wed 4 p.m. –midnight, Thu–Sat 4 p.m.–1:45 a.m.

D'Vine Wine Bar, 836 W. St. Clair Ave., Cleveland, (216) 241-8463

Get in-line

When summer hits, **IN-LINE SKATERS** can be found at Mill Stream Run Reservation in the Cleveland MetroParks, where skaters converge throughout the summer, creating their own community. It's the most skater-friendly spot in Cleveland. You can rent skates and pads here, and even take classes that will teach you how to stop, go, and eventually become an in-line whiz. After skating, mix and mingle with the crowd at the ice-cream stand, where skaters trade tips on where to find other good roads and trails around town. The Skate and Snack is open in the summer months Mon–Fri 8:30 a.m.–6 p.m., Sat 8:30 a.m.–5 p.m., Sun noon–5 p.m.

Mill Stream Skate and Snack, Mill Stream Run Reservation, 16200 Valley Parkway, Strongsville, (440) 572-9990

TIPS AND REMINDERS

When you're at a party, look for people who seem like they're not having a good time and introduce them around.

Go on a blind date

Squeamish about blind dates? No need to be. Call **LUNCH DATE**, a service that will connect you with other like-minded people and set you up for a low-pressure lunch date. If you like the person, schedule a longer date. If not, no harm done. It's an interesting way to meet people, especially if you're a busy professional, or a little bit skittish about the personal ads. All you have to do is call up and fill out a questionnaire, and Lunch Date will do the rest.

Lunch Date, 812 Huron Rd., Cleveland, (216) 687-8139

Mongolian horde

Brian Diehl, marketing manager at North Coast Logic, is among the more gregarious Clevelanders I know. His favorite stop for socializing with strangers is the **MONGOLIAN BARBEQUE**. "It's not your average restaurant. You have to get up and move around to prepare your own, and wait with other folks while it is being cooked," explains Diehl, adding, "these are all great chances for striking up conversation." Mon–Thu 11 a.m.–10 p.m., Fri–Sat 11 a.m.–11 p.m., Sun 11 a.m.–8 p.m.

Mongolian Barbeque, 1854 Coventry Rd., Cleveland Hts., (216) 932-1185

Lend a helping hand at camp

Miss the fun of summer camp? Volunteer to be a **COUNSELOR** at Camp Cheerful, designed for campers up to age 21 who have Muscular Dystrophy. Volunteers are needed to assist summer campers with activities throughout the day and night. Contact the MDA to find out how you can volunteer.

Camp Cheerful/Muscular Dystrophy Association, 16600 W Sprague Rd # 190, Cleveland, (440) 816-0916

If you're going to bar hop . . .

Recent college grads mingle with fortysomethings in an odd display of brotherhood on Thursday nights at the **WEST END BARS** in Lakewood. This ritual has long been going on in the "Tri-Bar" area, as locals call it, as partyers travel between a collection of bars along Detroit Road that includes the Riverwood Café, where a live band plays R&B, to another place just around the corner—called Around the Corner. The close proximity of these joints makes it easy to play a game of social leapfrog, inviting potential future dates to the next stop and seeing if they follow. The joints get so crowded with people that you're almost forced to talk with cuties all night long. What a bother! The Tri-Bars are open daily 5 p.m.–2:30 a.m.

West End of Lakewood, at 185th and Detroit Ave., Lakewood

Be a part of the show

Want to be part of the action? Let **PLAYHOUSE SQUARE** make an instant actor out of you. Their annual production of *Flanagan's Wake* requires that playgoers become part of the play. The show, which usually runs in the fall, is a live-action wake where audience members play the parts of the mourners. You'll be seated with strangers and meet new people in a theatrical environment. Be sure to order tickets in advance.

Playhouse Square Interactive Theatre, Playhouse Square Center, Cleveland, (216) 241-6000

Alternative night spots

Been looking for a place to show off your new belly-button ring? Explore your **ALTERNATIVE** side by dancing and socializing at the Cage, and Fridays and Saturdays are particularly popular. The music is noisy, the atmosphere dark, and the crowd cool. Meek-hearted or conservative types should stay at home, but if you want to see the other side of Cleveland, this is the place to go.

The Cage, 9506 Detroit Ave., Cleveland, (216) 651-0727

Cycle with a group

Join the Cleveland Touring Club, a **RECREATIONAL CYCLING CLUB** with approximately 200 members of all ages and riding abilities. They host year round regular weekly and weekend rides, as well as occasional rides to area festivals and events. The rides are loop rides, so you end up in the same place you start out, and each ride offers two to three distances for you to choose from, ranging from 25 to 65 miles. You can ride at your own place, and you're bound to hook up with a someone who goes just your speed. Yearly dues are a bargain at $15 for individuals and $20 for families, and include subscription to their monthly newsletter, *Crankmail*, invitations to special social events, and more. Call about membership and to get a riding calendar.

Cleveland Touring Club, (440) 954-4201

Alternatives:
Lake Erie Wheelers (touring & racing), (440) 779-8392
PDQ Cleveland (racing), (440) 235-4458
Western Reserve Wheelers (touring), (216) 751-4977

Be a Latin lover

Sample the **LATIN MUSIC SCENE** at the Tropical Lounge, where the salsa beat takes over the dance floor—and you. Though any weekend night at Tropical Lounge ensures a dancing crowd, booming Latin music, and perspiring partiers, Wednesday at 7:30 is the time to come for Street Salsa lessons. For a small fee, instructors will guide you through the basics of this style of dancing. Learn all the moves with the instructors as your guides, dance the evening away with your classmates, then return on a weekend night and show off your new moves.

Tropical Lounge, 3382 W. 44th St., Cleveland, (216) 651-0870

Tea for two . . . or more

Craving some civility during the holiday season? Attend a Victorian tea in November at the Coulby Mansion. Moms, how about inviting your daughter, her best friend, and her best friend's mom to make this a holiday tradition? It might even catch on with other moms in the neighborhood. It'll be just you and the girls at a **FASHION SHOW**, listening to Christmas carols and nibbling on small cakes, and meeting others in the civilized set.

Coulby Mansion, 28730 Ridge Rd., Wickliffe, (440) 943-7100

Please talk during the movie

At Talkies, the mocha is bittersweet, the conversation flows, and movies are always playing. You'll never be lonely in this coffeehouse that features a friendly coffee-bar atmosphere as well as a small **SCREENING ROOM** where films play day and night. Weekend nights are especially lively at this Ohio City neighborhood joint because resident film buff Bill Guentzler picks the flicks and works the crowd, bringing customers together with coffee and reels. Mon–Sat 7 a.m.–10 p.m., Sun 8 a.m.–8 p.m.

Talkies Film & Coffee Bar, 2521 Market Ave., Cleveland, (216) 696-3456

Mingle at the marathon

Runners: let your favorite sport become a full-blown mission, and meet people in the process. The annual **CVS MARATHON** in May might seem an unlikely place to meet someone, but think again. While training for a marathon, you could quite literally run into people, and on the day of the event, the support you get from other runners can create strong bonds. One woman I know got two dates running a marathon! Call to register for the race in advance; it starts at 7:30 a.m.

CVS Marathon, downtown Cleveland, (800) 467-3826

Get jazzed

Jazz aficionados don't miss the **JAZZ ON THE CIRCLE SERIES**, which brings the best jazz performers to Cleveland for some horn-blowin', guitar-strummin' good times. Such legendary performers as Dave Brubeck and the Dizzy Gillespie All-Star Alumni Band have played at venues that include Severance Hall and the Cleveland Museum of Art. Stick around after the shows to meet the artists—and Cleveland's most dedicated jazz fans, who hang around to mingle. Tickets are sold individually, but purchasing a series pass will help you get to know the who's who of the Cleveland jazz scene.

Jazz on the Circle Series, (216) 791-2909

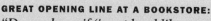

GREAT OPENING LINE AT A BOOKSTORE:
"Do you know if (insert local library name) has a book club?"

Go out on first night

Looking for a place where families get together on New Year's Eve? Come to **FIRST NIGHT AKRON**, a New Year's Eve party that takes over the streets of downtown. The focus is on family-oriented events that are fun for the whole crowd. Arrive early so that you can try all the food, play every game, get every face painted, and finally, count down every second to the new year. There is no admission fee; the event runs from 6:30 p.m. to 12:30 a.m.

First Night Akron, downtown Akron, (330) 762-8555

Patronize the arts

Arts and crafts fans congregate annually at the **CAIN PARK ART FESTIVAL** in July. Artists gear up for this event with glee, because it's in such a nice setting and so well attended. Patrons and browsers casually make their way through the artists' stands, talking about the creations on display and trying to get a bargain on a favorite piece. There's also lots of food to eat and entertainment that includes a children's choir performance.

Cain Park Art Festival, Cain Park, Lee and Superior Rds., Cleveland Hts., (216) 291-5792

The *real* place to be on St. Paddy's Day

Anyone who tells you that a good place to meet someone is at a bar on St. Patrick's Day hasn't been to church that same morning. Before the parade, revelers arrive hours before **MASS AT ST. COLEMAN'S** in Ohio City to claim a seat in a pew for mass. Enjoy mass—this is where all the fife and drum corps go before the parade—then join the caravan downtown to stake out a spot on Euclid Avenue. There is no better matchmaker than the mother of an Irish bachelor or bachelorette, and if you announce your availability, you could conceivably have a date every day for the rest of the month. The church doors open at 7 a.m.

St. Coleman's Church, 2027 W. 65th St., Cleveland, (216) 651-0550

TIPS AND REMINDERS

Take a risk. If you see someone who looks
interesting, don't listen to those voices in your head
that give you 10 reasons not to talk to the person.
Walk up and say "Hello."

A don't-miss affair for amateur food critics

Cleveland's die-hard foodies come together at the Nautica Entertainment Complex every fall at **A TASTE OF CLEVELAND**, where everyone's a food critic for the day. Chefs from around town offer the best from their menus for Clevelanders to sample, and proceeds go to charity. Why not invite someone you meet at this event to join you at a favorite restaurant to sample their full menu? Call for the dates and to order tickets.

A Taste of Cleveland, (call Belkin for tickets (440) 247-2722)

Roll in the hay

Bring a friend and meet some others on a **HAYRIDE** at Lake FarmPark. Groups of 15 or so get cozy on the ride, singing camp songs together without shame. And hot cider and hot chocolate follow each ride, affording you an opportunity to fall for the cutie with the straw in his hair. Call Lake FarmPark between 8 a.m. and 5 p.m. to get this year's hayride schedule and to sign up for a ride.

Lake FarmPark, 8800 Chardon Rd., Kirtland, (440) 256-2122

Circle the Circle

Every December **UNIVERSITY CIRCLE** opens its collective doors to the public for free. Families enjoy the opportunity to prowl museums at no cost, and almost every arts institution offers special events for all ages. University Circle Fest is a good opportunity for single parents to meet and mingle. Call for date and times.

University Circle Fest, (call University Circle, Inc. for information (216) 791-3900)

Lounge on the lawn

A pleasant, sociable crowd turns out to hear the Cleveland Orchestra play at **BLOSSOM MUSIC CENTER** during the summer. Why not join in? In fact, why not buy season tickets and invite a new friend each time you go? Arrive early to socialize before the concert and bring a basket of your favorite foods. Also bring a durable blanket to sit on and an extra sweater. If you attend more than a few concerts, you'll start recognizing and getting to know other patrons as you borrow extra napkins. Call for a schedule and to buy season tickets.

Cleveland Orchestra at Blossom Music Center, 1145 W. Steels Corners Rd., Cuyahoga Falls, (216) 231-1111

Mix with classical music buffs every week

Looking for friends who share your love of classical music? Join the Akron-based **TUESDAY MUSICAL CLUB** to hear classical music while meeting an active group of people who share your passion. Every Tuesday this group meets at social hours and lectures, held before and after classical music events. You can also attend dinners and after-concert soirées with other club members once you get to know them. Call to find out when and where the next meeting will be.

Tuesday Musical Club, 198 Hill St., Akron, (330) 972-2342

One of Ohio's largest cultural festivals

Join Akron's African-American community at the **AFRICAN AMERICAN CULTURAL FESTIVAL AND PARADE** in July. This celebration has been going on for more than 20 years and attracts upwards of 20,000 people from all over the region, including thousands from Cleveland. Activities for kids and adults highlight a day of fun, food, and festivity. If you want to make new friends, volunteer well in advance to help organize the event. Call to volunteer and to find out event dates and times.

African American Cultural Festival and Parade, Lane Field, at Wooster Ave. and Moon St., Akron, (330) 762-8723

Taste the NFL

Why not invite that BROWNS FAN from the office you've been wanting to get to know to join you at Taste of the NFL? You'll mingle with the stars and fans of the NFL, eat fancy food, and donate money to charity when local chefs team up with the league to bring this event to the fans. The location varies from year to year; call for schedule and tickets.

NFL/Cleveland Browns, (440) 891-5050

Meet the greek community

Where can you meet some Greeks? At Tremont's annual **GREEK FESTIVAL** in May, when Cleveland's tight-knit Greek community throws opens its doors and invites everyone to a party. The food is extraordinary, and the dance floor is where you'll want to spend most of your time. Greek music is lively and complicated, and each dance is exciting to watch and try. Learn as you go, seek out a kind soul who can teach you the steps, and dance off all that baklava. Call for festival date and times.

Greek Festival, Church of the Annunciation, 2187 W. 14th St., Tremont, (216) 861-0116

Join high society for a night

If you'd love to get all gussied up, attend a big bash, and fraternize with Cleveland's elegant set, plan to attend the **JUMP BACK BALL** in February at Playhouse Square. This isn't an ordinary party—it's a monster of a party complete with dancing, live music, gambling, a fashion show, a silent auction, and Cleveland's young and up-and-coming dressed in their finest and eager to get social. Call for date, time, and to order tickets.

Playhouse Square Partners, 1501 Euclid Ave., Cleveland, (216) 771-4444

The arts fest that's more like a block party

People seem to do more chatting than buying at the **CLIFTON ARTS FESTIVAL**. For a few days in June, a humble section of Clifton Avenue becomes the site of a bustling neighborhood arts show, as artists and musicians sell their wares and entertain the crowds in a flurry of activity. People are extra friendly during this neighborhood get-together, so it's easy to go alone and make new friends. Call for festival dates and times.

Clifton Arts Festival, at Clifton and 117th Sts., Cleveland, (216) 228-4383

Meet Cleveland's canine community

Dog enthusiasts shouldn't miss this opportunity to mingle with **CLEVELAND'S CANINE ELITE**. Dog owners and fans take over the I-X Center every December for the Crown Classic, a truly spectacular dog show. The small cost of admission is worth it, as you'll see all classes of dogs competing while observing the range of emotions the owners and trainers go through as they compete for "best in show." Stick around and mingle with the crowd here that shares a common devotion to man's best friend. Call for a show schedule.

Crown Classic Dog Show, I-X Center, 6200 Riverside, Dr., Cleveland, (216) 676-6000

Build castles in the sand

Professionals, students, and beach bums all come together for the annual **SAND CASTLE TOURNAMENT** at Edgewater Park. This is the Iron Man competition for sandcastle builders. Many architecture and engineering firms and students plan for months to compete here. Walk around as the competitors work through the day, and get to know this interesting crowd. The tournament runs from 9 a.m. to 3 p.m; call for the date.

Sand Castle Tournament, Edgewater Park, 3600 John Nagy Blvd., Cleveland, (216) 881-8141

For classical music fans with pianist envy

Music aficionados and legends of the piano world converge on Cleveland for a few days every other August at the Cleveland International **PIANO COMPETITION** at the Cleveland Institute of Music. Tension is high, but the thrill of competition brings the crowd together and gets conversations flowing between performances. Call CIM for competition schedule and tickets.

*Cleveland International Piano Competition/*Cleve. Institute of Music, 11021 East Blvd., Cleveland, (216) 791-5000

Party at an art auction

Cleveland photographer Dan Morgan has an inside scoop on meeting art scene devotees: "Become a fixture at SPACES. The best opportunity for meeting and greeting happens around Halloween, when SPACES hosts Cleveland's hottest **ART AUCTION AND COSTUME PARTY**. Purchase a ticket to the dinner, meet the artists, and bid on the art. Or go the route of the budget conscious and show up after dinner to browse the art and the crowd." Call for date; the event runs from 6:30 p.m.–midnight.

SPACES Gallery, 2220 Superior Viaduct, Cleveland, (216) 621-2314

For the insatiably curious—you have a lot to learn

If you love learning, you've got to register for the next **EXPLORER SERIES** at the Cleveland Museum of Natural History. These lectures investigate everything from dinosaur dung to photography to the great expanse of the universe. Pay a little extra for a boxed dinner that comes with the event, and you'll have an opportunity to get social about science. The series runs from September through May at 7:30 p.m. on designated days. Call to register and get the schedule.

The Cleveland Museum of Natural History, 1 Wade Oval Dr., University Circle, Cleveland, (800) 317-9155 x 279

Get tropical with the Hispanic community

Get familiar with Cleveland's growing **HISPANIC COMMUNITY**. A fun way to get involved is to attend the annual "Navidad Tropical" party at the RainForest in December. The party is a benefit for Esperanza, Inc., an association for Hispanic youth and families in greater Cleveland. If you really want to get involved, volunteer for a board committee; even if you just help set up for the party, you'll get to mingle with others while supporting an excellent cause. Call to volunteer and find out party date and time.

Navidad Tropical, Cleveland Metroparks Zoo, Cleveland, (Call Esperanza, Inc. for information (216) 651-7178)

Keep a tradition alive

Read to kids or tell them stories as a member of the Cleveland Association of **BLACK STORYTELLERS**. They offer classes and events to help you get to know the other volunteers; some of them are storytellers by trade. Get involved by volunteering to read to a class or a children's group. The more animated you are, the more popular you'll be with young audiences—and they always want just one more story.

Cleveland Association of Black Storytellers, (216) 991-0230

Get to know urbanites

Love gritty, urban neighborhoods and the people who live there? Then the TRENDY TREMONT Arts & Cultural Festival is the event for you. The mix of cultures—ranging from new artists to fixtures in the Polish community and everything in between—makes this a special event, filled with loud music, good food, and cutting-edge artwork. The festival is held in September; call for exact dates.

Tremont Arts & Cultural Festival, W. 14th and Starkweather, Tremont, (216) 575-0920

Right place, right time—the grocery after work

One of the best area grocery stores for meeting single professionals is **HEINEN'S** Rocky River location, where many stop on their way home from work. Don't be afraid to strike up a conversation with someone who looks interesting. They may be taking home dinner for one. Mon–Wed 8 a.m.–8 p.m., Thu–Fri 8 a.m.–9 p.m., and Sat–Sun 9 a.m.–6 p.m.

Heinen's, 19219 Detroit Rd., Rocky River, (440) 331-3830

Become a master of the toast

Here's a way to build confidence and friendships all at once—join **TOASTMASTERS**! The local chapter, at CWRU, welcomes new members who want to learn to be more confident and comfortable in public speaking and in social situations. Think of it as a place to meet people who can help develop your people-meeting skills. Guests are always welcome to participate or simply observe. Club meetings are held every first and third Tuesday of the month from noon–1 p.m.. Feel free to just show up.

CWRU Toastmasters Club 8711, Dental School Enlow/Gould Seminar Room, CWRU, Cleveland, (216) 368-4649

Join a team of amateur scientists

Volunteers work in small groups **ASSISTING MUSEUM CURATORS** prepare materials for exhibit at the Cleveland Museum of Natural History. For example, one group works in the paleobotany department cataloging plant fossils and preparing slides for the curator so she can study them under her microscope. Volunteers are trained on site. It's an excellent opportunity to learn—and to acquire new "colleagues."

Curatorial Assistance Program/Cleveland Museum of Natural History, 1 Wade Oval Dr., Cleveland, (call the Volunteer Coordinator, (216) 231-4600 x349)

Share SPACE with Cleveland's artists

Get to know our town's young art community: Volunteer at **SPACES GALLERY**. Whether you're hanging a show or pouring drinks at an opening, you'll have an opportunity to meet and talk with Cleveland's up-and-coming artists and some of this town's most generous and enthusiastic patrons. Call to join a committee or sign up for any small job. Open Tue–Fri 11 a.m.–5:30 p.m., Sat 11 a.m.–5 p.m., Sun 1 p.m.–5 p.m.

SPACES Gallery, 2200 Superior Viaduct, Cleveland, (216) 621-2314

Hoop it up

Think you're pretty good with a basketball? Then hoop it up! For a few crazy days in August, this town is swarmed with three-on-three teams competing for charities at the **HOOP IT UP TOURNAMENT**. Beginners and all-stars alike can participate in the fun—or just people-watch—as hundreds of competitors hit the courts for a cause. All the proceeds from this event benefit local charities. If you don't play basketball, join in as a volunteer to help coordinate the event or get people from place to place. Call to volunteer and get dates, locations, and tickets.

Hoop It Up, downtown Cleveland/Flats, (216) 420-2000

Join a brew-ha-ha

Cleveland's beer lovers gather downtown every April at the **MIDWEST BREWFEST**. There, you can taste hundreds of varieties of brew and compare notes with other beer lovers all day long. The convivial atmosphere here delights patrons, who travel from booth to booth sipping and learning about their favorite beverage. Plan to take a cab home. Call for a schedule and to get tickets.

Midwest Brewfest, Cleveland Convention Center, 500 Lakeside Ave., Cleveland, (440) 247-2722

Hands-on fun for antique car lovers

About 70 volunteers meet Wednesday evenings to help maintain and restore the wonderful **ANTIQUE CARS AND AIRPLANES** in Crawford Auto-Aviation Museum. They do everything from spit-shine fenders to repair engines. No prior training is necessary; you just have to like old cars. The group right now is mostly men, but the museum would love to have more women take part.

Crawford Auto-Aviation Museum/Western Reserve Historical Society, 10825 East Blvd., Cleveland, (call the Collections Manager, 216-721-5722)

If your love life's cold, put on a hat

At the annual **HATS OFF TO THE WAREHOUSE DISTRICT** Party, hats serve as the best icebreaker you can imagine. Since its inception—the party honors milliners who worked in the warehouse district 100 years ago—this has been one of the most fun parties of the season. (It's also a must-attend function for any seriously social single looking for a mate.) Attendees are encouraged to design and wear creative hats; prizes are awarded for the best. Held in April; call for the date and to order tickets.

Hats Off to the Warehouse District Party, Warehouse District, downtown Cleveland, (216) 344-3937

The don't-miss neighborhood party

Crowds are packed in during the **FEAST OF THE ASSUMPTION** in Little Italy, so mixing and mingling is the order of the day as you learn new dances, sample liqueurs, and make new friends. Among Cleveland's best-known ethnic festivals, the Feast celebrates Italian culture, Catholicism, and cuisine. Come and walk through the galleries of Murray Hill, take a spin on a carnival ride, taste the bounty of Italy, and drink grappa with the diehards. You'll leave begging for more. The feast takes place in mid-August; call to find out the exact dates.

Feast of the Assumption, Murray Hill, at Mayfield Rd. and Murray Hill, Cleveland, (216) 231-8915

TIPS AND REMINDERS

If you're the new person at a business function or professional organization meeting, arrive early and ask a member to introduce you around. That's the best time to meet the other members, and you won't feel quite so anonymous during the meeting.

Stay late

If you go to the museum only for the art,
you're missing the AFTER-HOURS FUN. Every
Wednesday and Friday night during the summer, the
museum stays open until 9 so visitors can look at art,
mingle, and people-watch. Munch on offerings from
the museum café, listen to music, and mill around with
the crowd, and you will meet a hip set of young and
old who enjoy culture and breezy nights
in the museum courtyard.

Cleveland Museum of Art, 11150 E. Blvd., Cleveland, (216) 421-7340

Watch the burly men

Looking for a burly man? You'll find him at the annual **OHIO SCOTTISH GAMES** in June. Men in kilts play bagpipes—some of the best pipe bands in the region compete here—while others throw bails of hay or even telephone-pole-sized logs through the air. The lively music and entertaining events have the whole crowd chatting together before the day is through. Call for dates and times.

Ohio Scottish Games, Oberlin College campus, Oberlin, (440) 442-2147

The holiday bash recommended for singles by singles

This is one party where you're almost sure to make a new friend. In fact, **SCROOGE'S NIGHT OUT** is a favorite annual event for singles, who meet as they sample foods from Cleveland's best restaurants, listen to live music, and gamble at the mini-casino. Hundreds of partygoers make this one of Cleveland's most successful fund-raisers. Prizes are awarded throughout the night, and silent auction items often make great entrees to future dates. Scrooge's Night Out is held one evening in December from 6 p.m.–1 a.m.; call for the date and to order tickets.

Scrooge's Night Out, Cuyahoga Valley National Park, Grays Armory, 1234 Bolivar Rd., Cleveland, (216) 621-5938

The mother of all rib fests

For three or four days in May, master barbecue chefs and those who worship their creations head downtown for the Cleveland **RIB COOK-OFF**. There's a cornucopia of ribs for sampling, beer to wash 'em down with, and music to dance to when you think you can't move another inch from eating so much. If you love this sort of thing, also check out the Rib 'N Rock cook off in Parma. Call for dates and times.

Cleveland Rib Cook-Off, Burke Lakefront Airport, downtown Cleveland, (440) 247-2722
Rib 'N Rock Rib Cook Off, 5255 Regency Dr., Parma, (440) 886-1700

Get your oompas out

Like oompa bands, bratwurst, and weitzen beer? Join this **GERMANIC ORGANIZATION** and meet others who do, too. With more than six events every month, this club stays active, hosting dances throughout the year, a New Year's Eve party and, of course, an Octoberfest with all the trimmings. Get on the group's mailing list and attend an event with some friends, or bring the kids along for one of the many family-oriented events hosted by the group.

Donauschwaben's German-American Cultural Center, 7370 Columbia Rd., Columbia Township, (440) 235-2646

Meet other dedicated Tribe fans

Autograph hounds know that attending the Cleveland Indians **AUTOGRAPH PARTY** is the best way to boost the value of their trading cards on e-bay, and it's the best place to trade secrets with other autograph hounds. Meet team members and impress a friend by getting a coveted autograph from a favorite player. If you really want to be on the inside track, call the Cleveland Indians and volunteer to help with the event. Call for autograph party date and times.

Cleveland Indians Autograph Party, (216) 420-4200

A very social sushi bar

The Ritz-Carlton isn't as stuffy as it used to be, especially at the **CENTURY RESTAURANT**. The sushi bar overlooking the Avenue is a great place for people - watching and -meeting. On weekend nights, grab a seat at the bar and chat with other patrons about what to order, or which sake to try. Live music in the lounge adds to the lively atmosphere. Sun–Thu 6:30 a.m.–2 p.m. and 5:30 p.m.–11 p.m., Fri–Sat 6:30 a.m.–2:30 p.m. and 5:30 p.m.–midnight.

Century at the Ritz Carlton, 1515 W. 3rd St., Cleveland, (216) 902-5255

See double

Where do twins go to see and be seen? Twinsburg, of course—during the TWINS FESTIVAL in August. At this festival, twins of every size, shape, race, and creed show up to mingle with each other. They come from across town and across the world. Even if you're not a twin, it's fun to people-watch here, and interesting to hear twins talk about their twinhood. Call for festival schedule.

Twinsburg Twins Festival, 10075 Ravenna Rd., Twinsburg, (330) 425-3652

Revel in sisterhood

If you're a young African-American woman, check out the **SISTER CONVENTION**, put on in the spring by WZAK FM. It showcases products and services targeted just to you. Conferences and lectures are designed to build a sense of community and strength among the crowd. Plan to spend a significant amount of time here, and you'll have a chance to make connections among the who's who of Cleveland's African-American community. Call for a show schedule.

Sister Convention, CSU Convocation Center, Cleveland, (call WZAK for information (216) 621-9300)

The art walk everyone talks about

Those interested in staying on top of Cleveland's art scene become regulars at the **MURRAY HILL ART WALK**. The galleries and restaurants in Little Italy stay open late to cater to a friendly crowd of browsers and strollers. I like the buzz at the Murray Hill Schoolhouse, where a host of stores and galleries open their doors, creating a party atmosphere. The Art Walk happens on the second weekends of June, October, and December.

Murray Hill Arts Association, at Murray Hill and Mayfield Rd., Cleveland, (216) 721-4100

The easiest day to meet tree-huggers

Meeting fellow environmentalists is easiest on Earth Day—particularly at **EARTH FEST** at the Cleveland MetroParks Zoo. Rest assured that the crowd at this event is kind-hearted, liberal-minded, and world-oriented. This event, which celebrates all things natural, draws hundreds of volunteers—also known as clean-up crews—who conduct random acts of kindness across the city and educate youth about recycling and taking care of our planet. Be a volunteer and an activist with the Earth Day coalition, and you'll be in with the in-crowd on Earth Day in April. Call to volunteer and get a schedule.

Earth Day Coalition's Earth Fest, Cleveland MetroParks Zoo, 3900 Wildlife Pkwy., Cleveland, (216) 281-6468

GREAT OPENING LINE AT A COFFEE SHOP:
"Do you know where they keep the Free Times and Scene around here?"

Dress for success

Get involved in a cause that will have you working with **WOMEN HELPING WOMEN**. Founded on the principal that you can't get a job if you don't have a suit to interview in, Dress for Success helps low-income women get into the workforce by providing them with suits to wear to interviews. You'll work on clothing drives and fund-raisers while expanding your sisterhood in Cleveland. Call to volunteer.

Dress for Success, 1303 Prospect Ave, 3rd Floor, Cleveland, (216) 781-3372

But even they probably can't refold a road map

A small but enthusiastic group of cartography buffs meets two to four times a year for programs about **MAPS AND CARTOGRAPHY**. The Northern Ohio Map Society rotates meeting locations west, east, south, and downtown to accommodate all members. Past programs featured visits to mapmakers, a demonstration of GPS equipment by a surveyor, and a talk by the head of the Map Division of Library of Congress. There are about 100 members; from 12 to 30 show up for each meeting. It's an informal group, and there's no membership fee.

Northern Ohio Map Society, (call Maureen Farrell, Cleveland Public Library Map Collection, (216) 623-2880)

Go on that blind date . . .

Don't get too frustrated when your friends and family try to set you up with someone. Their hunch might be right. And even though **blind dates** can be scary, sometimes they really do pay off, like in the case of Rose and Wally Griffith: "Rose had just come back to town from college, and was trying to make new friends in the Cleveland food scene," Wally says. "She befriended my father and stepmother, Fred and Linda Griffith, who set us up on a blind date. I wasn't too excited about it at first, but the date lasted until about 4 a.m. Within six weeks we were married."

Fund-raise on foot

More than 6,000 people converge on downtown streets to raise money for the **MARCH OF DIMES WALK AMERICA** event each summer—and guys, more than half of them are women aged 25 to 54. Why not join them? Spend a few weeks before the walk gathering sponsorship donations from co-workers, neighbors—even strangers. This lets you finally say "hello" to that accountant in human resources you've always wanted to meet. On the day of the event, walk three to six miles to raise the money, then join in on an all-afternoon party to celebrate raising more than $450,000 for charity. Call to sign up for the walk.

Walk America, Public Square, downtown Cleveland, (call March of Dimes for information (216) 518-1663)

Hobnob with the wine snobs

Every August, wine snobs unite at **VINTAGE OHIO** at Lake FarmPark in Chardon. Ohio is among the major grape-producing states, and its wines win international competitions every year. Taste for yourself by sipping on Ohio vintages and nibbling on fresh Ohio cheese. This event draws a sophisticated crowd that enjoys an opportunity to mingle and talk wine. Call for event schedule and to order tickets.

Vintage Ohio, Lake FarmPark, 8800 Chardon Rd., Kirtland, (440) 256-2122

Hundreds of Irish eyes a-smilin'

Nothing encourages sociability like a few pints of beer—at least that's the philosophy at the **IRISH CULTURAL FESTIVAL** in July. As pipers pipe and kind-hearted women serve up corned beef sandwiches and soda bread, you'll mingle with Cleveland's Irish. Near the end of the festival, the party-goers make plans to continue the festivities at nearby pubs, so stick around for the late-night fun, too. You may be planning an Irish wedding soon. Call for festival schedule.

Irish Cultural Festival, Berea Fairgrounds, Berea, (216) 251-1711

Running for women

Every September, more than 17,000 runners commit to **RACE FOR THE CURE**, a breast cancer fundraiser. Some are survivors of breast cancer, and many more have lived through the experience with a family member or a friend, but all are joined by the common goal of raising money to find a cure for this illness. If you're not a runner, participate by helping to hand out T-shirts or water, or just stand near the finish line to cheer the runners on. Call to volunteer or sign up for the race; the race goes from 7:30 a.m. to 4 p.m.

Race for the Cure/Susan G. Gorman Breast Cancer Foundation, 10819 Magnolia Dr., Cleveland, (216) 791-2873

Have an art attack

Come to the **CLEVELAND CENTER FOR CONTEMPORARY ART** on the last Friday of every month from 7 p.m. to 9 p.m. While Starbucks coffee brews, the hip and trendy art set gathers to see dance, music, and performance art for a fee of only $5. Mixing and mingling is easy; the art generates lively conversation and opportunities to meet someone who shares your interest in all things hip.

Final Friday of Every Month, Final Fridays Café, Cleveland Center for Contemporary Art, 8501 Carnegie Ave., Cleveland, (216) 421-8671

Join the league

If you're under 35, consider getting involved in the **YOUNG CITIZENS LEAGUE**, an active group that seeks to bring young people into the political and governmental arena. The Young Citizens League is sponsored by the powerful Citizens League of Cleveland, and active young professionals are recruited to assist with the many luncheons sponsored by the parent organization, or to add some life to the networking parties they host. Call to find out how to get started.

Young Citizens League, 1331 Euclid Ave., Cleveland, (216) 241-5340 ext. 10

Help haul in the harvest

If you've got kids, attending the **LAKE FARMPARK HARVEST FESTIVAL** is a great way to meet and socialize with other families while learning first hand about life on the farm. Kidless? Bring some nieces and nephews to this family-oriented event, and you'll meet friendly folks while you work on the farm, watch the work dogs strut their stuff, and milk cows. The festival is held in September; call for a schedule.

Lake FarmPark Harvest Festival, 8800 Chardon Rd., Kirtland, (440) 256-2122

Team up to build a park

Volunteer to help revitalize an urban space. **PARK WORKS** builds playgrounds in urban settings and restores existing parks and other spaces for public use—and they need help. Call the office to volunteer for a day, and you might help an area school install a learning garden that will be used for years to come. Projects typically use 50 to 100 volunteers and take the better part of a day to complete. Come on your own, or bring friends and officemates. Call to sign up as a volunteer.

Park Works, 1836 Euclid Ave. #800, Cleveland, (216) 696-2122

Dress like a rock star

If you like rock and roll, even remotely,
you'll be guaranteed a good time at the Rock and Roll
Hall of Fame's ANNUAL HALLOWEEN BASH. Those who
attend the party dress to the nines—many of them
decked out like their favorite rock stars—and dedicate
the evening to music, dancing, and cavorting around.
Call for date and times.

Rock and Roll Hall of Fame and Museum, 1 Key Plaza, Cleveland, (216) 781-7625

Frolic with the flower children

Smile on your brother—and the biggest assortment of hippies you'll see all year—at the **HESSLER STREET FAIR**. The sixties come alive at this annual event, when people young and old in tie-dyed shirts take over the street to meet, greet, dance, and commune. The Hessler Street Fair is the place for counterculture lovers to get a jump-start on the summer festival season. Happens in May; call for schedule.

Hessler Street Fair, Hessler St., University Circle, Cleveland, (216) 556-3716.

Meet the art formerly known as prints

Be there on the first Friday of every month when **ZYGOTE PRESS** presents hand-pulled prints and artwork. Cleveland's art enthusiasts converge here, and if the shows seem more convivial than many such events, perhaps that's because the prices are affordable, and they hardly ever run out of beer. Look for Liz Maugan, one of the founders of the gallery, whose favorite hobby is playing matchmaker to her guests. She'll make sure you meet someone new. The shows run from 5:30 p.m.–7:30 p.m.

Zygote Press, 7209 St. Clair Ave., Cleveland, (216) 881-4000

Show up for a show at high noon

Spend lunchtime doing something social when the **SHOWTIME AT HIGH NOON** series kicks off during the summer. Tri-C brings performances and lectures to various locations downtown for noontime programs that last about an hour—to keep you out of trouble with the boss. Because of the casual daytime atmosphere, it's a great place to meet new people. Perhaps you'll find someone to share your walk back to the office. Call for a schedule and to sign up.

Showtime at High Noon, Tri-C Metro Campus, 2900 Community College Ave., Cleveland, (216) 987-4127

Help find a cure

Meet a dedicated group of caring volunteers, health-care professionals, and local AIDS activists who join forces on December first, **WORLD AIDS DAY**. Local activities include concerts, benefits, and a daylong program at the Health Museum that creates awareness and raises money for the World AIDS Foundation. Call the Health Museum to find out how you can get involved—pass out flyers, greet patrons, or help set up events.

World AIDS Day Program, Cleveland Health Museum, 8911 Euclid Ave., Cleveland, (216) 231-5010

Local history buffs unite!

A grand gathering for **LOCAL HISTORY BUFFS** is held every October. The Western Reserve Studies Symposium sounds a little imposing, but actually "It's easy. Really easy," according to organizer Gladys Haddad, professor of American Studies at Case Western Reserve University. The 2-day event brings together academic and non-academic speakers and an enthusiastic general audience for a series of presentations followed by group discussions. About 200 or so attend. It's held either on the CWRU campus or at Squire Vallee Vue Farm, depending on the theme.

CWRU, (call Gladys Haddad, (216) 368-4117)

Ring it in on the Square

Ring in the new year with a family crowd on Public Square. Cleveland's **NEW YEAR'S EVE CELEBRATION** includes ice skating, live music, and fireworks at midnight. New Year's Eve on Public Square runs from 6 p.m.–12:30 a.m.

New Years Eve on Public Square, Public Square, downtown Cleveland, (216) 664-2000

The equestrian event of the year

The horsey set in Cleveland does know how to throw a party, and if you're interested in horses (or the people who own them), you should be sure to check out the **HUNTER JUMPER CLASSIC** at the MetroParks polo field in July. This event draws a healthy mix of enthusiasts and diehards who enjoy the beauty of the beasts as much as the competition itself. Stick around for the entire show and angle for an invitation to a postshow party. Call for a show schedule.

Hunter Jumper Classic, MetroParks Polo Field, Moreland Hills, (440) 834-8615

Be a kid again

Make a bold visual statement and see who notices, at the **CHALK FESTIVAL** at the Cleveland Museum of Art in September. Buy a spot on the sidewalk and a box of chalk from the museum for $15, then scribble to your heart's content. If you really want to really impress the crowd, attend chalk art workshops offered in the weeks prior to the event. The kids and families that attend get acquainted as they visit each other's chalk creations. Call for festival date and times.

Cleveland Museum of Art, 11150 East Blvd, University Circle, Cleveland, (216) 421-7340

Fall for art

ART BY THE FALLS brings visitors out in droves to mingle, buy art, and enjoy the carnival foods of summer. More than 100 artists converge on Cuyahoga Falls for this festival held amidst lovely weather and a picturesque setting. It's among the first arts festivals of the summer season, with live music that brings a light, friendly mood to the people. Art by the Falls happens in June; call for a schedule.

Art by the Falls, Riverfront Center at Front St., Cuyahoga Falls, (440) 247-7507

Be a stonewaller

If you're a member of the gay community and are disenchanted with ordinary party politics, consider joining the **STONEWALL DEMOCRATS**. This group supports national political platforms that promote the interests of gays and bisexuals. The Cleveland chapter is also very active locally. Join this group and become an activist while meeting the politically aware in Cleveland's gay and lesbian community. Call to find out the next meeting time and location.

Stonewall Democrats, (216) 647-7437

Get some pub culture

Fashioned after traditional Irish pubs in Dublin, this little bar in the Flats is a hot spot on weekends, but Sunday mornings are an even better time to meet someone here. A full Irish breakfast is served as patrons watch televised European football games. If you're attracted to accents, a trip to **FADO** on a Sunday morning or afternoon will be pleasing to your ear as displaced Irishmen and other Europeans stop in to catch the games. Mon–Sat 11 a.m.–2:30 a.m. and Sun 11:30 a.m.–midnight.

Fado, 1058 Old River Rd., Cleveland, (216) 771-0066

Haul out the sap

It may sound corny, but singles and families alike come to the Geauga County **MAPLE SUGAR FESTIVAL** in droves to haul in sap. Find out what life was like when syrup came out of a tree instead of a glass granny, and get to know your fellow workers. After a morning filled with work, sit down to a communal meal of sausage and pancakes slathered in lovely maple syrup. The festival takes place in late winter; call for dates and times.

Geauga County Maple Sugar Festival, Geauga County Fairgrounds, 14373 N. Cheshire St., Burton, (800) 775-8687

Share a day of music

You'll find no better opportunity to run into culturally minded folks who love our city's orchestra and its beautiful performance hall than at the **ANNUAL DAY OF MUSIC**. This October event is popular with music fans of all ages. It's a thrill to walk through Severance, see what it's like backstage, and listen to live performances—of all kinds of music—for free. The Annual Day of Music runs from 10 a.m.–7 p.m.; call for exact date.

Severance Hall, 11001 Euclid Ave., Cleveland, (216) 231-1111

Go to the Garden Party

The **GARDEN PARTY** is likely the biggest event of the year in the gay community, featuring live entertainment, silent and live auctions, a luncheon buffet, raffles, and socializing. Tickets are $40, and worth every penny for this upscale and fun event. Guests dress to the nines, and the food is excellent. The Garden Party takes place in July; call for date and time.

Lesbian/Gay Community Center, location changes annually, (216) 651-5428

Politically active doctors

If you're a doctor looking to meet a doctor, look no farther than **PHYSICIANS FOR SOCIAL RESPONSIBILITY**. This group gets active in global issues on a personal level by lending their support to local causes. They organize rallies, promote awareness campaigns, and meet to discuss issues of the day on a regular basis. Call to find out when and where the next meeting will be.

Physicians for Social Responsibility, 1919 E 107th St., Cleveland, (216) 721-2470

A little seltzer down your pants

Cleveland Public Theatre's **VAUDEVILLE SHOW** in December has the best tagline in town: "A little song, a little dance, a little seltzer down your pants." It's fun to attend this madcap show—some acts are astounding for their accuracy and flair, while others are hilariously bad. If you really want to get to know the cast and regulars, sign up ahead of time to be a part of the show—just call them to schedule an audition. But even if you come just to watch, get caught up in the camaraderie of the crowd and make a new friend to go to the theater with.

Cleveland Public Theatre's Vaudeville Show, 6415 Detroit Ave., Cleveland, (216) 631-2727

Where everyone's in the holiday spirit

At 6 p.m. on the day after Thanksgiving, join merry Clevelanders ushering in the holiday season. The **HOLIDAY LIGHTING CEREMONY** at Public Square is a tradition for hundreds of families who come from all over greater Cleveland to attend. The city puts on a great, family-friendly show with ice-skating, live music, and a brilliant light display. The crowd is very sociable as they huddle to try and keep warm. Call City Hall for the annual schedule of events.

Holiday Lighting Ceremony, Public Square, Cleveland, (contact Cleveland City Hall (216) 621-4110)

Become a notary public.

This is a great **NETWORKING TOOL** for professionals like lawyers, accountants, and financial planners—especially if you've recently set up your own practice. Often, people find out at the last minute that they must have important personal or financial documents (wills, 401K transfers, deed transfers) notarized—but don't know a notary public. Advertise your availability as a notary (a simple bulletin-board notice or a small ad in trade publications might suffice), and some of them will come to you. To become a notary public in Cuyahoga County, you must be a resident of the county and a registered voter. Fill out an application, pay a $30 fee, study a manual, pass the test, wait a few weeks for your certificate . . . and you're off and notarizing. You get to use a cool stamp, too. For more specific instructions, call the Notary Commission Office.

Notary Commission Office of Cuyahoga County, *Old Courthouse Building, 1 Lakeside Ave., Room 101, Cleveland, (216) 443-8623*

Share Kwanzaa

The annual **KWANZAA FESTIVAL** at the First Community Interfaith Institute explores ancient and new traditions in the African-American community, bringing families together for a celebration of culture. Parents will enjoy an opportunity to meet each other while children dance to African drumming and traditional music, and listen to folk tales. Bring the family. The festival runs from December 26 to January 1; call for a schedule of events.

First Community Interfaith Institute, 142 Cleveland St., Elyria, (440) 366-3244

Go formal

Increasingly, this is becoming an event for singles to attend, but single or no, the black-tie **RED CROSS BALL** is your once-every-two-years' chance to meet Cleveland's who's who in the elegant setting of the Renaissance Hotel Ballroom. If you are single, request a seat at the singles table when you make your reservations. If you don't have success at your table, meet and greet as many attendees as you can; there's always a married couple playing Cupid. The ball is held in winter, every other year; call for date and time.

American Red Cross, (216) 431-3010

Look up an old friend . . .

Remember your old high school sweetheart? Ever wonder what they're up to these days? It never hurts to get in touch, and just maybe there's a chance to **rekindle old flames**. It worked for Jonathan and Michelle Kish: "Me and Michelle grew up together and always talked about the day I'd be a chef, she'd be a doctor, and we'd be married," John says, "After college, I came back to Cleveland to open the Inn at Turner's Mill, and she came in from out of town. When I saw her at the restaurant, I thought, 'Oh, no, here comes trouble.' But we started dating. And soon after, on a vacation in Tahoe, I said to her, 'Hey, you wanna get married today?' That was it."

Parade the Circle

You can meet people at **PARADE THE CIRCLE**, but to see what they look like you might have to take off their masks. This unusual celebration has a theatrical bent, as Cleveland emulates New Orleans for the day, and attendees dress in extravagant costumes for this parade. If you want to get really into it, volunteer to help plan the event and get costumes and floats ready for the parade. Call to find a volunteer position or get event date and time.

University Circle Inc., 10831 Magnolia Dr., Cleveland, (216) 791-3900

Talk turkey

Want to enjoy Thanksgiving dinner without all the guilt? Start the day off with some exercise at the **TURKEY TROT** run. It's invigorating to be out in the brisk November air with a few thousand Clevelanders who can choose to run a full five miles or walk just one. Go at your own pace, find a partner, and vow to meet again to walk off the holiday weight gain and stress. The Turkey Trot happens on Thanksgiving Day at Burke Lakefront Airport; call for details.

Turkey Trot Fun Run, (call Hermes Race Systems for information (216) 781-6411)

Meet Clevelanders outside Cleveland

You can actually meet a lot of Clevelanders by getting out of town for the weekend. Try a **BED & BREAKFAST**. Local travel writer Doris Larson says that in the course of researching her book, *Bed & Breakfast Getaways from Cleveland*, she met lots of interesting Clevelanders staying in cozy quarters under the same roof. She suggested the Charm Countryview Inn, in Charm, Ohio, where breakfast is "a major happening." They serve a big Amish feast at a communal breakfast table—you can't help but meeting your fellow guest while passing them the hash browns. (Doris's book describes another 79 B&Bs to try, too.)

Charm Countryview Inn, 3344 S.R. 557, Charm, (330) 893-3003

Watch out for buzzards

It's amazing, but people actually show up to watch the **RETURN OF THE BUZZARDS** every year. More amazing, though, is what a great time this can be. Revelers gather early to catch a first glimpse of these unattractive flying meat-eaters in the early morning hours of March 15, then the people return on the 18th to put on a festival in honor of the birds.

Hinckley Buzzard Festival, Hinckley Reservation, off Bellus and State Rds., Hinckley, (216) 351-6300

"Eat, eat!"

Italian cooks or epicureans looking for a bargain on bulk basil make their way to **GUST GALLUCCI'S** on Saturdays. The shopping here is great, but it's almost as much fun to get a slice of hot pizza and people-watch for a little while. Since there are so many food fans in the aisles, it's easy to get a conversation going—gather opinions on the virtues of Asiago cheese, or plot a dinner party menu with an expert stranger. Open Mon–Fri 8 a.m.–6 p.m. and Sat 8 a.m.–5 p.m.

Gust Gallucci's, 6610 Euclid Ave., Cleveland, (216) 881-0045

Mingle with serious poetry lovers

It's not widely publicized, but world-class poets travel to Kent State University throughout the academic year to deliver lectures and read their work to students, faculty, and other guests. You'll have a chance to mingle with area **POETRY ENTHUSIASTS**—and even the poets themselves—at the post-discussion punch bowl. The series is a great way to mix couplets, so mark your calendar in advance. Call for series dates and times and to register.

Wick Poetry Center at KSU, Satterfield Hall, Kent State University, Kent, (330) 672-1772

Share womanhood

Women take over the I-X Center for a few
days in September to learn about everything to do
with womanhood—from lipstick to feminism,
it's all here at the EVERYWOMAN SHOW. If you're
looking to make new friends, this is a great place
to be. The show encourages a warm sisterhood,
and showcases plenty of activities designed for
and by women. Call for a show schedule.

Everywoman Show, I-X Center, 6200 Riverside Dr., Cleveland, (216) 676-6000

Get to work

Art McKay, who works at the Chanel counter at Saks Fifth Avenue, is a diehard believer in retail. His sure-fire way to make new friends goes like this: "Get a **PART-TIME JOB** in a retail store that you like. You'll be in a situation where you meet a lot of people—shoppers, co-workers, and employees at other stores. It's a fabulous way to meet friends of friends, too, and the opportunities keep growing—as do your opportunities for discounts. Plus, whomever you meet, at least you know they have a job."

A most extraordinary dance company

Volunteer to help an innovative dance company, **DANCING WHEELS**. Most of the dancers are wheelchair-bound, and attending performances really isn't enough—with the loss of the Cleveland Ballet in late 2000, this group needs financial support and manpower. Call them up and volunteer to do almost anything. You'll join a cast and crew that puts on some of Cleveland's most creative original productions.

Dancing Wheels, 1501 Euclid Ave., Cleveland, (call the G.G. Greg Agency for information (216) 692-1193)

Where people share a passion for raw fish

You never know who will like sushi, that addictive Japanese dish that combines fresh raw fish with hot flavors. But at the sushi bar at **GINZA** you'll meet a mish-mash of Clevelanders who share this common bond. The sushi bar here is especially lively on weekends, and if you tell the hostess/owner that you're single, she might just try to set you up with another customer. Mon–Thu 11:30 a.m.–2:30 p.m. and 5 p.m.–9:30 p.m., and Fri–Sat 5 p.m.–10:30 p.m.

Ginza Sushi House, 1105 Carnegie Rd., Cleveland, (216) 589-8503

Grant a wish

A lot of talent, effort, and creative thinking goes into **GRANTING WISHES** for children with life-threatening illnesses. Be a part of this dedicated circle of volunteers who help bring dreams to children each year. Volunteer to raise funds or assist with the many details that go into granting hundreds of wishes a year in Greater Cleveland. Marriages have been sparked by such activities, as do-gooders are often attracted to one another. Call to volunteer.

The Make-A-Wish Foundation of Northeast Ohio, 24100 Chagrin Blvd., #125, Cleveland, (216) 464-7755

Sail with the singles

You don't necessarily need to know how to sail to go sailing. Owners of racing sailboats need crew members to help staff their ships for early Sunday morning sails, and the **NORTH COAST SAILING SINGLES** can help you get on board. You really get to know folks when you spend so much time and effort working on a sailing team, and the after-race parties thrown by this group allow sailors to wind down and meet each other in a casual setting. Call to get your sailing assignment.

North Coast Sailing Singles, (216) 252-0177

See why it's it

Walk into **IT'S IT DELI** and you get the sense that everybody here knows each other. Deli food and homemade comfort food make this a great stop for a casual lunch, and you won't feel strange if you're on your own. Patrons don't mind if you invade their space a little to see the art on the walls just over their tables, and conversations frequently start up in the ordering line. Breakfast is especially social, and if you frequent this spot more than casually, you'll soon get to know the regulars. It's It serves breakfast and lunch daily.

It's It Deli, 11520 Clifton Blvd., Cleveland, (216) 651-3078

Go to a grand old Party

If your politics lean toward the right,
you have a home in Cleveland. May I suggest
the Republican Party headquarters as an
excellent place to find fellow REPUBLICANS in
Cuyahoga County? Plan fund-raisers,
welcome visiting dignitaries to town, and
plan more fund-raisers once you get involved
in the party. Call to volunteer.

Republican Party of Greater Cleveland, 526 Superior Ave., Cleveland, (216) 621-5415

Get turbo-charged

The **SPORTS CAR CLUB OF AMERICA** promises two kinds of bonding—the male kind and the body frame kind. You'll probably encounter both when you join this club, which allows members to show off their cars while they network for parts, or trade up for prestige. Auto shows throughout the year give car enthusiasts something to look forward to, and a forum for showing off. Attend workshops and learn how to race cars, or just follow the club's racing schedule for the real excitement. Call for the next meeting time and location.

Sports Car Club of America, (440) 331-5902

Be someone else's eyes

Read to those who can't see. The **CLEVELAND SIGHT CENTER** needs volunteers to read newspapers for those who can't. Try it a few times, and if you like it get involved with the center. From October through December, the Cleveland Sight Center gears up for an annual fund-raiser and a holiday greeting card sale. During this time, the level of activity is high, and selling the cards to friends, family, and strangers will get you out into the community. Call to find out how to get started.

Cleveland Sight Center, 1909 E. 101st St., Cleveland, (216) 791-8118

Learn to kid around a little

Got a great routine? Can you teach kids how to juggle? Share your talents with **YOUNG AUDIENCES OF GREATER CLEVELAND**. This organization matches people with a talent for teaching or performing with groups of kids who love to learn and play. They're looking for storytellers, jugglers, and theatrical types who have worked, or desire to work, in front of young audiences. Sign up for the group by contacting the office and attending meetings.

Young Audiences of Greater Cleveland, 10819 Magnolia Dr., Cleveland, (216) 421-7222

The event wine lovers wouldn't think of missing

When the new **BEAUJOLAIS WINE** comes in from France in November, get to the Market Avenue Wine Bar for a taste and to hear opinions from the knowledgeable and friendly staff and patrons. Conversations will flow in this congenial, thinking-person's bar, while the fragrance of the new Beaujolais hangs in the air. Call to find out the arrival date. Open Sun, Tue and Wed 4 p.m.–midnight, Mon 6 p.m.–midnight, Thu–Fri 4 p.m.–1 a.m., and Sat 2:30 p.m.–1 a.m.

Market Avenue Wine Bar, 2526 Market Ave., Cleveland, (216) 696-9463

Be a friend

If you're a fan of literature, you'll find a welcoming group of friends at the Cleveland Public Library. Become a **FRIEND OF THE CLEVELAND PUBLIC LIBRARY**, and you might be sent out to lend books at fun events around town, or asked to read to children on Saturday afternoons. The library gang is a friendly group, interested in getting the word out about the many services offered by their organization. Call to volunteer. (Or check out the "friends" group for your local library.)

Friends of the Cleveland Public Library, 325 Superior Ave., NE, Cleveland, (216) 623-2800

Make 'em laugh

Aspiring comics have been clamoring to take a class at the famous **SECOND CITY STUDIOS** on Prospect Avenue. You're almost guaranteed to meet other funny people there while you learn skills that will advance your status as the life of the party. Since the classes last four to six weeks, you'll get to know your classmates and teachers—and nothing creates a stronger bond than making a fool of yourself in front of near strangers, which you will do often and with glee. My advice: sign up on the first available day because classes fill up quickly. Call for a schedule.

Second City, 811 Prospect Ave., Cleveland, (216) 685-0100

Grow a your networking opportunities

If you're trying to move up the corporate ladder in Cleveland, you'll need to network. As Cleveland's largest networking and business organization, the **GREATER CLEVELAND GROWTH ASSOCIATION** is one of the few organizations listed in this book that can help you meet people *and* get you a discount on office furniture. Although there's a hefty fee for joining—around $500—the price of admission is well worth it for the small businessperson. In addition to frequent social hours and networking parties, membership in this group provides access to lawyers, accountants, and business professionals who volunteer time to helping foster the growth of small businesses in Cleveland. If you own a small business or want to network, this is the group for you.

Greater Cleveland Growth Association, 200 Terminal Tower, Cleveland, (216) 621-3300

GREAT OPENING LINE AT A GROCERY STORE:
"The produce is so much cheaper at the West Side Market."

Connect with computer users in person

Has anyone told you that you've been spending way too much time in front of the computer screen? Maybe you should check out the GCPCUG. As one of the oldest, biggest, and most influential computer groups in the country, the Greater Cleveland **PC USERS GROUP** commands a lot of attention from the industry, allowing them to host big shots for lectures and social events. The group, anchored by its founder, Dan Hanson, is a social organization as well. You can join the group formally by calling the office and getting on the list, or just show up for one of their events. The GCPCUG is one of those organizations that will make individuals who show up feel like they're part of the group, so don't worry about going on your own. And, by the way, there is probably no better place in Cleveland for a woman to have her pick of professional men. Call for the next meeting time and place.

Greater Cleveland PC Users Group, 3150 Payne Ave., Cleveland, (216) 781-8518

Is that a Pilot in your pocket?

Admit it. Since you got that Palm Pilot, you've become an addict, downloading every game available for this little gadget and yearning to learn about the secret shortcuts that only insiders know. Hot sync with others in the know by stopping in occasionally to chat with the **POCKET COMPUTING GROUP**. Nowhere in town will you get a phone number faster—or more accurately—than here, as you learn about computing with fellow Palm-aholics. They meet at Tri-C on the second Monday of every month from 6:30 p.m.–8:30 p.m.

Pocket Computing Group, Tri-C Eastern Campus, 4250 Richmond Rd., Cleveland, (440) 871-2532

TIPS AND REMINDERS

Go to church or temple. Really. Some places of worship
in the area seem to attract more single people
than others. Find out where these places of worship are,
and attend services there regularly.

Dance mysteriously

Can you imagine yourself dancing the mysterious and intricate dances of the Far East? The **ASSOCIATION OF ASIAN-INDIAN WOMEN** will help you learn this beautiful art. If you're good at it, you can aspire to perform with their award-winning dance troupe. The group, which performs throughout the city in an effort to raise awareness of Asian Indian culture, welcomes volunteers to help with their public appearances. Help with outreach events at area festivals, or attend dance classes.

Association of Asian-Indian Women, 3140 Essex Rd., Cleveland, (216) 932-0864

Loud music, lots of regulars

At the **GROG SHOP**, depending on the band that's playing, you might find a crowd of punk rockers, garage band geeks, folksy types, hippies, or frat boys. And then you have the regulars, who come here no matter what and fit in with any crowd. The place is no-frills, the drinks are cheap, the music is loud, and the people are cool. You'll have a good time and have lots of folks to talk to, no matter what night you come. Call for the band schedule. Daily 8 p.m.–2:30 a.m.

The Grog Shop, 1765 Coventry Rd., Cleveland Hts., (216) 321-5588

Bring your baby

Becoming a new mother can be scary and confusing. New moms should get to a **BABY & ME** group meeting, where you'll meet others in the exact same situation. Designed for moms with babies between 0 and 12 months, this group meets once a week to share, support, and learn. You'll make fast friends in this group where no one will frown on you for bringing baby along, and it's okay to talk openly about breast-feeding. Call ahead to confirm a meeting time, and show up at the classes on your own—the other mothers will welcome you with open arms. Baby & Me meets Wednesdays from 9:30 a.m.–11:30 a.m. and from 6 p.m.–8 p.m.

Baby & Me, Heights Parent Center, 1700 Crest Road, Cleveland Hts., (216) 321-0079

TIPS AND REMINDERS

Next time you're reading the entertainment listings and that voice in your head says, "Hey, I should go to that," pick up the phone and make plans before you forget.

Go fly a kite

If the childlike delight of flying a kite appeals to you, then make a point of spending an afternoon with some new friends from the **OHIO SOCIETY FOR THE ELEVATION OF KITES**, which meets Sundays at noon at Edgewater Park year round. Show up with nothing but two sticks, some newspaper, and a string, and within a half-hour, you'll have a kite flying through the air. Of course, if you want a real kite, you can pick one up at most drugstores during the spring and summer or at Wings Hobby Shop any time of year. Don't be shy about showing up on your own—or bringing the kids along. This friendly group welcomes everyone and is there to help you get that kite off the ground! They tend to go out for a bite to eat once they're worn out, and even host a potluck a few times a year. But best of all, they're friendly people. Meet them.

Ohio Society for the Elevation of Kites, (330) 274-2818
(meets at Edgewater Park Beach, 3600 John Nagy Blvd., Cleveland)

Wings Hobby Shop, 17112 Detroit Rd., Lakewood, (216) 221-5383

Go to even small dinner parties . . .

I hosted a dinner party so I could flirt with Francesco Melfi, a very good-looking professor from Italy. But I was tied up in the kitchen with a complicated dinner during most of the prime mingling time. That's when Francesco met Karen Marano. She was invited as someone else's date, but she fell in love with Francesco before I could serve the salad. The two lovebirds are living together in Cleveland Heights, and the fireworks are still going off. The moral: attend even the smallest of affairs. Take every opportunity you get to **meet new people**. It won't always end up in romance, but I bet you'll at least make a lot of new friends.

Pal up with a marathon runner

If you like competing in local runs and are getting to know the serious players at the marathons, it's time for you to train for the big one. Designed for serious runners, the **TOWPATH MARATHON** in October is the qualifying race for those who wish to compete in the Boston Marathon. While you're training, keep your motivation high by signing up to help organize the race—this will keep you on the inside track, so you'll know which high-profile runners are planning on attending and be provided with plenty of motivation to keep training. Call to sign up for the race.

Towpath Marathon, Cuyahoga Valley National Park, (216) 348-1825

A Crunch fan club with perks

If you're hooked on soccer, then maybe you already attend Cleveland Crunch games at the CSU Convocation Center. But did you know you can get extra perks by joining the **CLEVELAND CRUNCH BOOSTER CLUB**? The booster club organizes trips to away games, hosts special nights at home games, and raises funds for the team's charities. Kick around with some of our town's most avid soccer fans.

The Cleveland Crunch Booster Club, 4400 Renaissance Pkwy., # A, Warrensville Hts, (216) 896-1140

Be all business

Entering the business world after a few years in college ain't easy. Holding down a full-time job can really wreck your social life. Meet others facing the same dilemma through the **YOUNG PROFESSIONALS OF GREATER CLEVELAND**, a networking and social group for single professionals under 30. With a strong focus on social events, the group also gets involved in charity work and business seminars, allowing you to help someone or learn something while you get to know young, professional Cleveland. Call for information; meeting times and locations vary.

Young Professionals of Greater Cleveland, (216) 556-5242

Build on a foundation

Get in immediate and intimate touch with the Cleveland arts community by becoming a member of the **CLEVELAND ARTISTS FOUNDATION**. With its strong emphasis on promoting and celebrating local art, the foundation sponsors local exhibits, encouraging members to attend related lectures and parties. You'll get to know more about art, and meet culture fans and local artists in the process.

Cleveland Artists Foundation, 17801 Detroit Ave., Cleveland, (216) 227-9507

The mingling people take over the street!

Something wonderful happens to **Market Avenue** in the summer. The crowds at the bars on this short street take to the sidewalks with their beer, wine, mixed drinks, and coffee. A diverse mix of people streams out of the Market Avenue Wine Bar, the Great Lakes Brewing Company, the Flying Fig, and Talkies Film and Coffee Bar—but everyone seems to know each other as people cross the street to say hello. Merchants hope the city will one day close off the street to add to the festive atmosphere here, but in the meantime, look both ways before you go chasing after a friend—you'll make plenty while you're here.

Market Ave. and W. 25th St., Cleveland

Go for Baroque

Being a fan of Baroque music means you might have to work hard to find friends who share this interest. Well, they're probably already hooked up with **APOLLO'S FIRE**, Cleveland's very dedicated group of early music performers. In addition to putting on fabulous performances, this group hosts lectures and parties. Attend a lecture on your own to start meeting fellow fans, and soon you'll have friends to attend concerts with. Call for a concert and event schedule.

Apollo's Fire, 23811 Chagrin Blvd., Cleveland, concert venues vary, (216) 378-2850

You *will* dance at the Savannah

At the **SAVANNAH BAR AND GRILLE**, people dance—and they don't like to see anyone get left out. Bands here range from swing to jazz to rock, and regulars wear comfortable shoes for a night on the dance floor. Almost every night of the week, there's something happening here, and the regulars always stake their claims on the dance floor. You should, too. Open daily 10 a.m.–2:30 a.m.

Savannah Bar and Grille, 30676 Detroit Rd., Westlake, (440) 892-2266

A sweet spot for squash and racquetball

Finding a squash partner is easier when you join the **Cleveland Racquet Club**. The membership is a bit pricey, but well worth it if you like to play racquet sports year round—and they have workout facilities as well. The staff at the club will hook you up with other players and a court. They have facilities for racquetball and tennis, too. Tournaments held year round foster competition and camaraderie. The facilities here are first-rate, and the social scene is bouncing. Make the club a twice-weekly stop and you'll soon have your game in shape—and your social calendar filled out.

Cleveland Racquet Club, 29825 Chagrin Blvd., Cleveland, (216) 831-2155

A not-so-secret society of film buffs

If you like films, you really should join the **CLEVELAND FILM SOCIETY**. This well-run organization hosts parties, talks, classes, and fund-raisers throughout the year that will put you in touch with fellow film buffs at least once a month. Some of the best classes offered at the society's trendy Ohio City offices last for six weeks, allowing you time to really explore a film genre or learn more about screenwriting. Most people sign up individually, but wind up becoming part of a close-knit group. Call for a class schedule and calendar of events.

Cleveland Film Society, 2501 Market Ave., Cleveland, (216) 623-3456

Cavort with cooks

If you're a chef—or a serious fan of cooking—consider joining the **AMERICAN CULINARY FEDERATION**'s Cleveland chapter. You'll hobnob with Cleveland's brightest chefs while learning more about food, the restaurant business, and the secrets of the trade. Working the off-hours in the restaurant business can make your social life suffer, so give it a boost by meeting others who share your interests—and your strange hours.

American Culinary Federation, P.O. Box 5124, Willowick, (216) 621-2231

Meet the press

If you want to be a member of the press corps—or just rub elbows with those who are—consider joining the **PRESS CLUB OF CLEVELAND**. The club hosts frequent social and professional development programs for writers and communications professionals, and even organizes annual trips to a golf course and to Jacobs Field—for more professional development, of course. Newcomers are made to feel welcome at the group's social events, where you're sure to see a face you recognize from newspapers or TV. Just ask Lynn Bracic—the group's secretary who is almost always at the registration table—to connect you with a board member who can introduce you around at the party. Call for a schedule of events and to join.

Press Club of Cleveland, University Club, 3813 Euclid Ave., Cleveland, (440) 899-1222

> **GREAT OPENING LINE AT A BLOSSOM ORCHESTRA CONCERT:**
> *"Didn't I meet you at Severance last season?"*

Be in the dad club

If you're a dad living in Lyndhurst, I've got *the* club for you. The **Lyndhurst Dad's Club** promotes good sportsmanship and goodwill by sponsoring youth sports tournaments throughout the summer. Members serve as coaches, organizers, trainers, and even chauffeurs. The dads also put on banquets for the kids and special events for the community. Call to find out when and where the next meeting will be. If you're a dad living anywhere else, you should attend some meetings and find out how to start a dad's club in your community, because this is a great idea.

Lyndhurst Dad's Club, 5301 Mayfield Rd., Cleveland, (440) 442-2957

Help out at Ronald's house

Families of children with serious illnesses often stay at the Ronald McDonald house while their children are being treated. **VOLUNTEER** here, and you can help make their stay more comfortable and become a part of the Ronald McDonald House's large family of volunteers. Help in the office, the kitchen, or throughout the home on a weekly basis, or sign up to work at special events as an auxiliary volunteer. Call to find out how you can help.

Ronald McDonald House, 10415 Euclid Ave., Cleveland, (216) 229-5758

There's a costume contest, too!

Warm and fuzzy is the theme of the **WOOLLYBEAR FESTIVAL**. Tens of thousands of people visit Vermilion each October to see the parade and participate in this festival that honors the woollybear caterpillar. This event, championed by beloved Cleveland weatherman Dick Goddard, has grown over the years into one of the kitchiest events in the state. Dress up like a woollybear for the costume contest and strangers will come up to you and just start talking. Call for festival date and times.

Woollybear Festival, downtown Vermilion, (440) 967-4477

Have a friendly day

Here's a small treasure: attend **PUERTO RICAN FRIENDLY DAY**, and you'll discover Cleveland's Puerto Rican community in Tremont. Learn how to grill delicious plantains over an open fire, or taste sticky pastries. This lively event also features music, games for children, and an opportunity to get to know the Puerto Rican community. The festival is held in July; call for schedule.

Puerto Rican Friendly Day, Clark Field, Tremont, (216) 664-3528

Take a (challenging) hike

If you're a hiker who likes a challenge, sign up with the **NORTHERN OHIO HIKING CLUB**. The group will take you on a challenging hike—at least four miles and sometimes up to ten—through a different location every Sunday. If you're not in prime condition, choose a hike that's short and work your way up. Many of the hikers show up every week for exercise and the camaraderie that follows in the form of a hearty brunch. To find out more about hikes, visit the website and send an e-mail to the club president. Also check out the Cleveland Hiking Club.

Northern Ohio Hiking Club, www.geocities.com/hiking_ohio/, or
Cleveland Hiking Club, for info, send SASE to: P.O. Box 347097, Cleveland, OH 44134-7097

Row your boat

Ever dream of being part of a rowing crew? The Western Reserve Rowing Association will teach you how. This group works hard pulling their boats up and down the Cuyahoga River, and they play hard along the river's shores when the workout is done. They are always **LOOKING FOR ONE MORE ROWER**, so give them a call. If it's the off-season, ask for recommendations on training for the summer—you'll be glad you put in the extra effort after your first practice session.

Western Reserve Rowing Association, (216) 621-9772

For women who mean business

A business venue for women is what the **WOMEN'S CITY CLUB** provides. Supportive networking opportunities, great business contacts, and fun events are the hallmarks of this established Cleveland institution. By becoming a member, you'll have an opportunity to take workshops, attend networking lunches, and build strong relationships with businesswomen of all ages. Call for membership information.

Women's City Club of Cleveland, 1118 Euclid Ave., Cleveland, (216) 566-1011

Where the elite meet

Show up at **MOXIE** wearing your best clothes. This is a place to be seen. The crowd here is mostly 30-and-up, and on weekends they pack into the bar for drinks, waiting to be seated in the open, café-style dining room for an expensive meal. Spend some time in the lounge resting on a velvet couch, or rubbing elbows with Cleveland's business set. Open Mon–Thu 11:30 a.m.–2:30 p.m. and 5:30 p.m.–10 p.m., Fri 11:30 a.m.–2:30 p.m. and 5:30 p.m.–11 p.m., and Sat 5:30 p.m.–11 p.m.

Moxie, 3355 Richmond Rd., Beachwood, (216) 831-5599

Be a part of the Karamu family

Karamu House is a lot more than just a theater—it's an **ANCHOR OF THE COMMUNITY**. The Karamu complex is a home away from home for members of the African-American community, providing a place where kids, especially, can grow and learn. Volunteer here and share your talents to help kids learn the fundamentals of art, theater, and life. In the process, you'll meet other volunteers and become a part of Karamu's close-knit family.

Karamu House, 2355 E. 89th St., Cleveland, (216) 795-7070

For animal lovers

Join the Friends of the Cleveland MetroParks Zoo and you'll get SPECIAL PRIVILEGES, such as invitations to member parties, free admission to select events, and advance news of additions to the Zoo. Also, getting involved with this group will get you networking with other animal lovers as you become a part of one of the most progressive zoos in the country.

Cleveland MetroParks Zoo, 3900 Wildlife Parkway, Cleveland, (216) 661-6500

Warm up to a cause

Help fellow Northeast Ohioans make sure all local kids have shoes on their feet, warm clothes on their backs, and coats that are worthy of the slushiest snowball. **SHOES AND CLOTHES FOR KIDS** is much more than a collection box for clothes. Participants throw fund-raising parties and silent auctions while doggedly pursuing donations of money and clothes. Once you're involved in a committee or a fund-raiser, you'll want to volunteer regularly to make a difference while being with others who want the same. Call to find out how you can help.

Shoes and Clothes for Kids, (216) 881-7463

Go Bucks!

Cleveland is home to thousands of OSU alumni. If you're one too, why not join the Ohio State University **ALUMNI CLUB** of Greater Cleveland? They sponsor monthly events that range from scholarship dinners to blow-out parties during football season. And even if you're not an official alum, you can still party with the Buckeye fans.

Ohio State University Alumni Club of Greater Cleveland, 5451 Broadview Rd., Parma,
(call the OSU Alumni office (614) 292-2281)

A-C-L-You

Lawyers often fall in love with other lawyers. And one place they meet is the **ACLU**. Volunteering means you'll take on or support cases for free, which means you'll also have networking opportunities in the courtroom. The group also hosts fund-raisers and programs throughout the year, and they need your help. Call to find out how to get involved.

American Civil Liberties Union, 1266 W. 6th St., Cleveland, (216) 781-6276

Join up with aspiring filmmakers

If you want to learn how to **MAKE FILMS**, join the Cleveland Filmmakers. This group has classes in everything from storyboarding to scouting locations to cine-matography during its annual conference and throughout the year. They host local experts and film business tycoons from New York, Hollywood, and Toronto for workshops, and throughout the year hopeful filmmakers get together to help each other on projects and learn the craft of cinema. Call for membership information.

Cleveland Filmmakers, 2501 Market Ave., Cleveland, (216) 623-3456

Explore your consciousness

Learn about magic, explore the mind sciences, or discover alternative lifestyles at the Association for **CONSCIOUSNESS EXPLORATION**. This laid-back club exists to learn, putting on events almost every month that appeal to the broader side of the mind. Spanning interests from juggling to alternative healing methods to New Age therapies, the association is sure to provoke in you a sense that . . . maybe there's more out there. You don't have to be a psychic—or even know how to juggle—to be a part of this group. Call them to find out when the next event is taking place and show up with friends or on your own. Members are open and inviting, so bring a good attitude and explore.

Association for Consciousness Exploration, 1643 Lee Rd., Cleveland Hts., (216) 932-5421

TIPS AND REMINDERS

Pay it forward. Each time you find a group of people you like, vow to bring someone new into the group as a karmic payback.

A center for Hispanic culture

Learn to speak Spanish, or master the steps of a traditional dance with a class at the **CENTRO CULTURAL HISPANO** de Cleveland. Located in Tremont, the Centro is a vibrant space where classes taught by locals give you a well-rounded exposure to the arts that make up Hispanic culture. You will meet people from every walk of life here—whether it's second- and third-generation Hispanics hoping to learn traditional dances or executives hoping to master the Spanish language. Stop in during business hours to get a list of classes and sign up.

Centro Cultural Hispano de Cleveland, 3200 Franklin Blvd., Cleveland, (216) 281-0109

Go Moon-doggin'

Nostalgic rock-n-rollers gather at the **MOONDOG CORONATION BALL**. Since the 1950s, this event has been reviving the sounds and dances that helped put Cleveland on the map. The ball remains one of the most fun tickets in town, promising a trip down memory lane for the older set that attends, and delivering plenty of danceable rock 'n' roll to the next generation of fans. The ball happens in March.

Moondog Coronation Ball, Gund Arena, 100 Gateway Plaza, Cleveland, (216) 420-2000

Be in a league of your own

In the traditional ladder of social success in Cleveland, the first rung is the **JUNIOR LEAGUE**. Throughout its history in Cleveland, the league has aided the advancement of many Cleveland women by fostering a sense of sisterhood here. More than 1,100 women are members, focusing volunteer efforts on such outreach goals as battling illiteracy, assisting victims of domestic violence, and promoting preventative health care. You'll plan plenty of parties and fund-raisers, and you will also make a difference in the community where it counts—and develop relationships here that you can count on throughout your career.

Junior League of Cleveland, 10819 Magnolia Dr., Cleveland, (216) 231-6300

CLEVELAND FACT

There are more than 500 charities in Cleveland where volunteers can network while helping others.

Meet a mogul among the moguls

Meet fellow skiers and get discounts on ski excursions when you join the Continental **SKI CLUB**, which has been operating in Cleveland for more than 30 years. When the snow starts to fall, these folks—all of them over the age of 21—grab their poles and head to the hills. After-ski parties help them thaw out. The club regroups in the spring for a picnic, gets together in the fall for a clambake, and sponsors additional events monthly. They meet at 8 p.m. on the second and fourth Tuesdays of every month; call for membership information.

Continental Ski Club, (440) 585-4750 (meetings held at the Tavern of Wickliffe, 29701 Euclid Ave., Wickliffe)

Wahoo!

If your love of the **CLEVELAND INDIANS** runs deep, you'll want to join the Wahoo Club. Membership has its benefits, like pregame behind-the-fence parties, special opportunities to travel to away games, and spring training packages. You can be sure of meeting others who share your love of the Tribe, and keep in touch with them throughout the year through the club's website, or write for information.

Wahoo Club, P.O. Box 221142, Cleveland, 44122, www.wahooclub.com

If you lean left

On any given night at **Democratic headquarters**, a group of about 20 people are consuming pizza and pop, and stuffing envelopes for hours. And guess what? It can be fun—gossip and political discussions swirl around the table all night. During campaign seasons, the office heats up with activity, and opportunities for meeting party loyalists abound. Join in on the fun and meet some energetic Dems. Call ahead to sign up for campaign work in your neighborhood, or request to work with a specific group—the Young Democrats is an excellent group for the under-30 crowd. Or just show up at headquarters when you see the lights on; they'll put you to work right away.

Democratic Party of Greater Cleveland, 1466 St. Clair Ave., Cleveland, (216) 621-9750

Pet a pet

Pet lovers unite under the umbrella of the **ANIMAL PROTECTIVE LEAGUE**, where there is much good work to be done. The most visible volunteer assignment is helping with animal adoptions at malls. Though it takes some training, trust, and commitment to earn your way into this job, it's a sure-fire way to meet new people once you get out there. Who doesn't like to pet a fluffy puppy or kitty? Call to find out how to become a volunteer.

Animal Protective League, 1729 Wiley Ave., Cleveland, (216) 771-4616

The place be seen meeting someone

On weekend nights, there's no place better to be seen than at **JOHNNY'S DOWN-TOWN**. The room is lush and full of mirrors that help you check out patrons without getting caught. Put on your best suit and spend happy hour here listening to the pianist, sipping on a drink, and capturing the attention of Cleveland's elite business crowd. Mon–Thu 11:30 a.m.–3 p.m. and 5 p.m.–10:30 p.m., Fri 11:30 a.m.–3 p.m. and 5 p.m. –11:30 p.m., Sat 5 p.m.–11:30 a.m., and Sun 4 p.m.–9 p.m.

Johnny's Downtown, 1406 W. 6th St., Cleveland, (216) 623-0055

Get oriented to the ultimate outdoor adventure

If you've been hiking, biking, rock-climbing, and camping, you're probably ready for the ultimate outdoor experience—survival courses. The first step is **ORIENTEERING**—the art of getting from one place to another without getting lost. The Orienteering Club will teach you the subtleties of finding your way with a compass. Classes are conducted under the guidance of professionals. Call find out where and when they meet.

Northeastern Ohio Orienteering Club, (440) 729-3255

Play at Playhouse Square

Meet Clevelanders interested in culture, and the arts at a day long free-for-all at **PLAYHOUSE SQUARE PALOOZA** every September. On this day, visitors can walk backstage at the theaters, try on costumes, apply makeup in dressing rooms, and attend dance classes on Playhouse Square's stages, all for free. Plan to participate in as many workshops as possible; this is where you'll meet others who share your interest, and get a chance to really interact with them as you learn a new dance or try your hand at stunt-fighting. Call for date and times.

Playhouse Square Foundation, 1501 Euclid Ave., Cleveland (216) 771-4444

Start a networking club for your profession

Call five people in town who work in your field. Ask each of them to invite five
more **NETWORKERS** to an informal get-together at a busy downtown bar that has a
good happy hour, like the Flat Iron Café. Pick a day once a month for the group to
meet, and—if you and the other founding members are good hosts and hostesses—
watch it grow. Once your group catches on, you'll have an ever-growing circle of
friends.

Flat Iron Café, 1114 Center St., Cleveland (216) 696-6968

TIPS AND REMINDERS

Keep it business. If you're interested in a colleague
—romantically—and you're not sure if the feeling is
mutual, climb on your high horse and keep it business.
If they're interested, they'll let you know. And if they're
not, you haven't risked a good business situation.

The best place to network with business leaders

If you're a business leader who likes to get involved, try the **Business Volunteerism Council** of Greater Cleveland. It can connect you with projects and organizations that need help. Joining will put you in touch with other active business leaders in the community and help you to broaden your own social group by becoming involved in something big. Call to get all the materials you need to become a member and get hooked up with the projects that interest you, and those where you'll be of the most help.

Business Volunteerism Council of Greater Cleveland, Tower City Center, # 950, Cleveland, (216) 736-7711

Mix it up with friends of Bill W.

Recovering alcoholics seeking community can attend mixers sponsored by **ALCOHOLICS ANONYMOUS**. The dances feature live entertainment and an opportunity to get to know others in the community outside of the meeting atmosphere. Because so many individuals show up at these events alone, group leaders and regulars will work hard to make you feel welcome, and they'll even ask you to dance. Contact the area coordinating office for the date, time, and location of the next mixer; they're held frequently by various chapters throughout Northeast Ohio.

AA Mixers, (216) 621-1381

Take the bus

Taking **PUBLIC TRANSPORTATION** regularly is one of the simplest ways to meet people. Plus, it's good for the environment. Take a bus to work and you'll ride with people who live where you live, work where you work, and keep a similar schedule to yours. Board the bus and sit next to someone who looks interesting. Conversation will be easy because you already have something to talk about—your destination. Call RTA for rates and schedules.

RTA Answerline, (216) 621-9500

The art museum's group for the younger set

Does a **SCAVENGER HUNT** in the Cleveland Museum of Art sound like fun? The museum's Young Friends group puts these on—and other social events, too. The group, for 21–40-year-olds, brings people together to foster awareness and appreciation of the museum's collections. They host monthly events and an annual gala fundraiser. There are plenty of opportunities to work together on committees and as museum volunteers. Call for more information.

Young Friends/Cleveland Museum of Art, 11150 East Blvd, Cleveland, (216) 421-7340, ext. 595.

Sing a song

Musicians gather to share their talents and their songs at "song circles" sponsored by the **CLEVELAND FOLK MUSIC SOCIETY**. These fun, casual events are held about once a month. If you play an instrument, bring it along; or just show up with your voice in tune. Be prepared to trade songs and join in. Attending regularly is a great way to immerse yourself in the folk music scene, and you'll soon find yourself humming new tunes wherever you go. Call ahead to find out when the next song circle is planned.

Cleveland Folk Music Society, 3008 Clinton Ave., Cleveland, (216) 771-0875

Make a reservation

Let somebody else do the hard work of lining of prospects for you. The **RSVP DINING AND SOCIAL CLUB** brings groups of singles together for small outings or larger social events. This club tends to be less intimidating than one-on-one dating services. Call to fill out a survey, and they will put you with a group of people who share your interests. They'll let you select when and where you go.

RSVP Dining and Social Club, (330) 334-0078

Get on board

Do you find skis a bit too stodgy? Sign up for one of the **SNOWBOARDING CLASSES** offered throughout the day at Boston Mills, and learn how to carve down the slopes. Once you've got the basics, start out down a gentle hill and pick up moves from other snowboarders. Call for a schedule of lessons. Open Sun and Sat 8:30 a.m. –11 p.m.

Snowboarding at Boston Mills, 7100 Riverview Rd., Peninsula, (330) 657-2334

Get on a rugby team

Want to play rugby? Join the Eastern Suburbs **RUGBY FOOTBALL CLUB**. They compete in regional tournaments, so if you're experienced, that helps. But the league is on constant lookout for talented rookies, too, and they'll be delighted to hook you up with practice games and help you develop your skills. The season lasts throughout the summer, with plenty of hard playing on the field, and hard partying at the club's favorite pubs. Sign up to play and get to know a group of tough cookies.

Eastern Suburbs Rugby Football, (216) 556-5589

Spend a happy hour

Twice monthly, the **LESBIAN/GAY COMMUNITY** meets in a casual happy hour atmosphere to network. This friendly group welcomes newcomers for cocktails and socializing. In addition to being an excellent social opportunity, the happy hours have a reputation as good business networking events. Call the Lesbian/Gay Community Center in advance to find out where the next one will be held—then all you need to do is show up.

Lesbian/Gay Community Center, 6600 Detroit Ave., Cleveland, (216) 651-5428

A friendly little small-town park

Sitting on the cannon at **POINT PARK** is a simple pleasure that Willoughby residents have known about for years. Bring a Frisbee or ball and glove with you, and see how quickly you can make new friends in this picturesque park. Sunny weekend days bring a sense of carefree delight, as pick-up games develop and runners take extra time with their stretching.

Point Park, *downtown Willoughby, (call Willoughby Parks and Recreation (440) 953-4200)*

Volunteer with the singles

Put in some volunteer work while meeting other singles. That's the mission of **SINGLE VOLUNTEERS OF NORTHEAST OHIO**. Choose events and projects that appeal to you, knowing that other singles will be participating, too. Whether you work on a one-day event or commit to a longer-term project, sit back and let someone else do the work of finding nice people for you to meet. Call to volunteer.

Single Volunteers of Northeast Ohio, *(216) 265-8677*

Be jolly

One way to meet people while spreading good cheer is to ring a SALVATION ARMY BELL during the holidays. You'll meet plenty of passersby in a friendly holiday mood. Call the Salvation Army to get set up—they'll train you, give you a bell, and let you to pick the locations and times that work with your schedule.

Salvation Army, 2507 E. 22nd St., Cleveland, (216) 861-8185

Be a part of some of Cleveland's best cultural programs

The Cleveland Cultural Alliance brings northeastern Ohioans together to learn about **ASIAN INDIAN CULTURE** through dance. This group sponsors ballet and other performances including original productions throughout the year. Call the Cultural Alliance to find out how to get involved, and they'll provide you with opportunities that range from helping ballerinas with makeup to manning information tables at some of Cleveland's best cultural programs. Meeting locations vary.

Cleveland Cultural Alliance, 10700 Deer Run Dr., Grafton, (440) 605-9948

A real-time discussion group

Log on to a lively discussion in cyberspace, then meet in person to keep the discussion going. **OPENSEWER.COM**, a national organization, hosts meaningful online conversation and intellectual discourse. It also has groups that meet — live — in cities across the country, including Cleveland.

Open Sewer, www.opensewer.com

Point and shoot

The **LAKEWOOD PHOTOGRAPHIC SOCIETY** sponsors more than 40 events through-out the season (mid-September through mid-May). It provides instruction to any-one with an interest in photography. You don't have to own a 35-millimeter camera to join the group, but it helps if you do. You'll learn how to work everything from 35-millimeter cameras to 4x5 view cameras, and they'll provide the equipment. If you get good at it, join in on competitions and shows sponsored by the group. The club meets Tuesdays at 8 p.m.; call to sign up.

Lakewood Photographic Society, 16024 Madison Ave., Lakewood, (216) 226-5882

Fight hunger

The massive effort put forth by **HARVEST FOR HUNGER** is a year-round commit-ment for volunteers, who help with fundraisers, get the word out about the organi-zation, and hand out bags of groceries to families in need. The holiday season marks the group's greatest time of need and is the perfect time to get involved. Call Harvest for Hunger, and they'll connect you with a group that needs your help.

Harvest for Hunger/Greater Cleveland Committee on Hunger, 1331 Euclid Ave., Cleveland, (216) 436-2200

Hit the bull's-eye

Like playing darts? Meet and play with other dart throwers from all over Cleveland by joining the **CLEVELAND DARTER CLUB**. It sponsors tournaments and outings. If you get really good, compete in the club's Extravaganza, an event nationally recognized for its size and the number of ace darters who travel to Cleveland to compete. Call the league to find out when their next gathering is, and show up to play.

Cleveland Darter Club, 2231 W. 10th St., Cleveland, (216) 671-2582

Get behind the scenes

Helping at a theater is an excellent way to apply or develop your theatrical talents, and meet fellow thespians in the process. The **SIGNSTAGE THEATRE** brings drama to the hearing-impaired community. They need volunteers who can build sets, help with costumes and makeup, and manage behind the scenes. Call to find out how you can help.

Cleveland Signstage Theatre, 8500 Euclid Ave., Cleveland, (216) 229-2838

Be a part of the chorus

If you're looking for an artistic and social outlet in the gay community, join the **NORTH COAST MEN'S CHORUS**. You don't have to read music, or even be a great singer—even if you're tone deaf, there's always a triangle that needs to be struck or bells to ring on cue. The chorus has three productions throughout the year, and it often participates in regional and national festivals. Call to sign up for the chorus, and they'll put you to work.

North Coast Men's Chorus, (440) 473-8919

Indy film lovers unite!

Ever want to make your own movie? Meet people who have done just that at the **OHIO INDEPENDENT FILM FESTIVAL**. The festival is a must for anyone into independent film, and a fantastic opportunity to meet some of our state's most creative new filmmakers. Contacts you make at this festival now might be Hollywood hot shots later, so bring your little black book and rub elbows. The festival takes place in November; call for a schedule.

Ohio Independent Film Festival, Cleveland Public Theatre, 6409 Detroit Ave., Cleveland, (216) 781-1755

Run for it

This running club hosts almost as many parties as fitness runs. The **CLEVELAND HASH HOUSE HARRIERS & HARRIETS** describe themselves as a drinking club with a running problem. It is a tight-knit group whose members have funny nicknames, but they welcome newcomers—they might even give you a nickname, too. The group sponsors runs on such a regular basis that they had to install a 24-hour hotline—call to find out when the next run or party is and just show up.

Cleveland Hash House Harriers & Harriets, (440) 954-6666

Take a pledge

If you wake up in every morning with Bob Edwards, then maybe you ought to support WCPN, the NPR affiliate in town. Organize a group of friends or officemates to help for a few hours during the spring and fall **FUND DRIVES**, and you'll meet other WCPN supporters. Continue volunteering and you'll be on the inside track to attend station-sponsored events that attract Cleveland's intellectual elite and sometimes radio personalities from NPR. Call to sign up as a volunteer.

WCPN 90.3 FM, 3100 Chester Ave., Cleveland, (216) 431-3200

Get Gaelic

If you like networking with other Irish folks, the **IRISH-AMERICAN CLUB** is well worth the price of admission. My favorite thing to do at the club is watch the Gaelic football tournaments on Saturdays or Sundays in the summer. The games bring out a rugged set of Irish bachelors who play in the league, and the after-game cookouts are a blast. Stop down with a few friends, and you'll soon be a fan of this unusual sport. If you want to attend an occasional event at the club without becoming a member, call to find out when the next one is and just show up.

Irish-American Club, 8599 Jennings Rd., Cleveland, (440) 235-5868

GREAT OPENING LINE WHEN YOU'RE OUT FOR A RUN:
*"I really prefer the trails on the Towpath—
have you been there yet?"*

Build something

Even if your talent with tools is limited to picture-hanging, your hands are much needed for a **HABITAT FOR HUMANITY** project, where you might also build the framework for new friendships. There are two ways to get in on this: get the company you work for to sponsor the construction of a new Habitat for Humanity home, or call the office and ask for an assignment. They will connect you with a project that you can work on and teach you what to do.

Habitat for Humanity, 7181 Chagrin Rd., Chagrin Falls, (440) 247-0255

For the tallest in town

There really is a club for everybody, and if you're a woman taller than 5'10", or a man stretching above 6'2", the **SKYSCRAPER CLUB** is for you. Though you don't have to be single, most of the members are, and there is no better place to find a partner who shares your view. Affiliated with Tall Clubs International, this group sponsors activities and excursions for the tallest in town. Call them to find out what their next activity is, and show up for an evening out where you won't have to stoop down to carry on a conversation.

Skyscraper Club of Cleveland, (216) 556-1494

Put your best foot forward

A group of folks have figured out how to make morning exercise routines a little more exciting. They call it **"VOLKSMARCHING,"** and these friendly folks enjoy brisk walks and lively conversation on nature trails. They welcome newcomers of all ages and abilities, and walks are scheduled frequently—several every week. Just call to find out where and when the walks are held, find one that fits your schedule, and show up ready to go.

Valley Vagabonds, (440) 777-6036

Hold a baby

Become involved at **PROVIDENCE HOUSE** by dropping off diapers or helping to change them. The babies here are born addicted to drugs or without caring parents—and they need your love. Don't worry about not having experience with at-risk babies: trained staff members will walk you carefully through each step. Whatever your level of commitment, you'll meet a group of caring people who have one of the toughest and most rewarding jobs.

Providence House, 2037 W. 32nd St., Cleveland, (216) 651-5982

Get on the task force

Join a group of dedicated healthcare professionals and other caring individuals in the **AIDS TASK FORCE** and become a vital part of the solution to the AIDS crisis in this country. The Task Force is in constant need of volunteers for duties that range from helping in the office, to assisting with home health care, to helping organize some of the most popular benefits in town. Though the work is sometimes hard, it's always rewarding. Call to volunteer.

AIDS Task Force, 2728 Euclid Ave., #400, Cleveland, (216) 621-0766

Become an addie

Join the **CLEVELAND ADVERTISING CLUB** and network with greater Cleveland's best and brightest advertising and marketing executives. It isn't just for ad pros—anyone who needs to promote anything can benefit from membership. In addition to monthly meetings, the club hosts semi-regular happy hours, and they always need help with their annual awards ceremony. By participating, you'll be on the inside track for hiring the best agency for your next project, while meeting a convivial bunch of creative types. Call for membership and event information.

Cleveland Advertising Club, (216) 241-4807

The ultimate in "power lunches"

If you like to know what's going on in town, get involved with the **CITY CLUB**. Though it is best known for its Friday lecture-luncheons, the City Club is also a social organization with very attractive headquarters. Join especially if you're an independent contractor or work-at-home type who wants to fraternize at lunchtime every once in a while. Lunches get crowded here all week as members gather to commune. Meeting rooms make it easy for you to schedule business conferences. Social events put on each month by the club ensure that you'll meet the other members and develop a community of your own downtown. The club is open Mon–Fri 8:30 a.m.–5 p.m.

Cleveland City Club, 850 Euclid Ave., Cleveland, (216) 621-0082

TIPS AND REMINDERS

Work in pairs. Find a friend who wants to get out there as much as you do, get dressed up, go out, and work the room together.

Dive in deep

Find new diving partners in **AQUA MASTERS**, a group of scuba divers who know what they're doing. Don't know how to dive? Take their six-week certification course. Then join trips to diving sites as near as the shores of Lake Erie and as far away as the Galapagos Islands. Call to sign up for the class or to join the club.

Aqua Masters Scuba Club, (216) 694-4774

For railway buffs

Railway buffs have plenty of potential compatriots in the Cleveland area. There are so many clubs and groups, in fact, that an umbrella organization, the Northern Ohio Association of Railway Societies, keeps track of them all. Call NOARS for a referral to a group in your area or special interest—from history to modeling. One unusual group is the Midwest Railway Preservation Society. They get together on Saturday mornings at the old B&W roundhouse on W. 3rd St. to to repair and restore **OLD STEAM ENGINES**. They welcome new members; no experience necessary, just enthusiasm.

Midwest Railway Preservation Society, 216-781-3629, www.midwestrailway.org
Northern Ohio Association of Railway Societies, (216) 687-6998

Host your own show

Ever fantasize about having your own TV show? Your dream is within reach. Contact Adelphia Communications, where the staff will work with you to get your show on the air. **PRODUCING A SHOW** isn't easy, so you'll need to recruit plenty of friends to help you. But once you get rolling, you won't believe how many people you'll get to know as you conduct research and interviews, produce the show, and maybe even become a local celebrity.

Adelphia Communications, 1350 Euclid Ave., Cleveland, (216) 771-1534

Meet jazz lovers all over town

Jazz fans who become a part of the **NORTHEAST OHIO JAZZ SOCIETY** quickly become aficionados, traveling to East Side, West Side, and downtown clubs with a growing group of fellow jazz fans, and listening to some of the finest jazz Cleveland has to offer. Call to get on their mailing list, and soon you'll be swamped with opportunities to listen to, learn about, play, and follow jazz in Cleveland.

Northeast Ohio Jazz Society, 4614 Prospect Ave #533, Cleveland, (216) 426-9900

Argue for the arts

For attorneys who want to meet artists (or other lawyers interested in the arts), try volunteering at **LAWYERS FOR THE ARTS**. This group of volunteer attorneys works to ensure that the rights of artists—who often can not afford expensive legal counsel—are defended. By joining this advocacy arm of the Cleveland Bar Association, you'll network with other lawyers who share an interest in the arts, and you'll get to know the local arts community on a personal level. Call to find out how to join.

Lawyers for the Arts/Cleveland Bar Association, 113 St. Clair Ave., Cleveland, (216) 696-3525

Artists' support group

The **CREATIVE WRITING WORKSHOP** is the place to meet artists of all kinds—musicians, performance artists, writers, and more—and a place to exchange ideas, and trade critiques. The workshop meets regularly, providing a social outlet and support base for aspiring artists, and also to work together on special projects that help bring art, particularly language arts, to Cleveland's youth. Call the organization to find out where and when the next meeting will be held.

Creative Writing Workshop, (216) 932-3650

Frequent the fund-raiser circuit

Once you attend a couple of fundraisers, you'll find you run into the same people over and over again. For example, the Center for Families and Children holds FUNDRAISERS regularly; if you go to a couple of them in a row, you'll likely meet others doing the same thing. That's how Heather and Gage Price met: "I met Gage at a Center for Families and Children Benefit called 'Clam, Jam, Thank you, Ma'am,'" Heather says, "Then I met him at a few subsequent fund-raisers for the same group. I didn't like him at first, but we kept talking and a year and a half later we were engaged." Inspired? Call the Center for Families and Children to find out when the next couple of fund raisers will be. Go to them all.

Center for Families and Children, 1469 W. 9th St., Cleveland (216) 241-6400

Laughter is a great ice-breaker

Cabaret DaDa **IMPROVISATION CLASSES** help you come out of your shell and develop your inner comic. Whether you're in it to become a stand-up or just to improve your timing, you'll gain something from learning the improvisational techniques used in acting and comedy. Classes meet for about six weeks at various times throughout the year at DaDa's Warehouse District Theatre. With 10 to 20 participants in each class, you'll meet plenty of other wiseguys, too.

Cabaret DaDa Improvisation Classes, 1210 W. 6th St., Cleveland, (216) 696/4242

Explore nature

Meet a group of down-to-earth folks who explore almost every aspect of nature from the smallest critters to the largest trees. Each season brings a new set of programs, lectures, and outings for the **NORTH COAST NATURISTS**. The group is very friendly and welcomes new members, so don't worry about showing up alone for a program. Call to find out where and when the next meeting is being held, and show up for an activity that interests you.

North Coast Naturists, 21422 Timber Oak Ct., Cleveland, (440) 238-6177

Publicize

To network with the people who keep the news rolling, the events happening, and the copy coming, attend a **PUBLIC RELATIONS SOCIETY OF AMERICA**–sponsored event. Certainly,it's an excellent organization to join if you're in the public relations industry, but small-business owners and not-for-profit folks who want to learn more about the publicity game should network here, too. Call to find out about membership or ask about the next event.

Public Relations Society of America, (440) 899-1112

Specialized networking

Get networking with Cleveland's do-gooders. Young professionals are especially at-tracted to volunteering for the **MARCH OF DIMES** because of the many programs that get them face time with community leaders. If you're interested in networking with a particular group of people—for instance, if you're a recent college grad looking to find a job in public relations—then request to work with committee spe-cific to your goals. The staff is particularly adept at matching talent with need.

March of Dimes, 5410 Transportation Blvd., Cleveland, (216) 518-1663

Be SPOKEN for

Cycling with a group is certainly more social. **SINGLE PEOPLE ON KAREFREE EXCURSIONS** (SPOKES) makes it easy to meet and ride by regularly scheduled rides of varying difficulty throughout the cycling season. Whether you're into a short, flat ride or a challenging trek over hill and dale, it's nice to have the support of a group. Call to get a list of scheduled rides, then just show up with your bike, ready to go.

Single People on Karefree Excursions, (330) 798-0921

Stick around

Find fellow hockey fans and meet other players at **CLEVELAND HOCKEY BOOSTER CLUB** meetings. Soon you'll be attending Lumberjacks games with fellow club members. The club hosts meetings and events throughout the hockey season (October through May) and the entire year. Get involved by volunteering at Lumberjacks give-away nights. Everybody likes to get something free, and you'll be very popular handing out these little gifts. Call for membership information.

Cleveland Hockey Booster Club, meeting locations and event times vary, (216) 420-2594

TIPS AND REMINDERS

My mother's advice: put some lipstick on, and brush that hair away from your face! It never hurts to look your best when you go out—even if you're just going down to the grocery store. You never know who you'll run into.

Take a stab at something new

Serious fencers join the **ON TARGET FENCING TEAM** to compete, and novices join to learn the basics of this exacting sport—they'll even let you borrow the proper equipment while you learn. It's a fun and active group that loves newcomers, and wheelchair fencers are encouraged to participate in most area clubs as well. Call ahead to find out when new members can practice, and they'll set you up with a time slot and a group member whose ability level matches yours.

On Target Fencing Team, 6333 Forest Park Dr., Cleveland, (440) 327-0808

Get serious about film

A community of film buffs come regularly to the **CLEVELAND CINEMATHEQUE** to see foreign and art films. People waiting to buy tickets strike up conversations with each other, and because so many of them come alone, you won't feel odd if you're dateless. More than 250 films from faraway countries, by new directors, and from the classic film files are shown here each year. Stop in to see a film and pick up the season schedule.

Cleveland Cinematheque, 11141 E. Blvd., Cleveland, (216) 421-7450

Mix it up with the real bargain hunters

The garage- and **YARD-SALE CIRCUIT** provides excellent opportunities for meeting people. Show up early and be as outgoing as possible—you may be bargaining for a new friend. The best place to go is Lakewood on Saturday mornings in the summer; you can't drive more than a few blocks along Clifton Boulevard without finding a good yard sale. Singletons troll these sales in hopes of finding the perfect bookcase for their apartment, or a great deal on a mismatched set of dining room chairs. You just have to be in the right place at the right time . . .

A friendly all-night coffee shop

If you're tired of the bar scene but want a place to converse and listen to good music, you should check out **COMMON GROUNDS**. As home to one of the best jukeboxes in Cleveland, this coffee shop is also a great hangout for young folks and nondrinkers. It fills up most nights with a friendly crowd getting buzzed on coffee and cigarettes. Fuel up and make friends. With flyers everywhere advertising the latest raves and alternative events, you'll always have something to invite a new friend to. Open 24/7.

Common Grounds, 17104 Lorain Ave., Lakewood, (216) 252-4768

Eat at Nate's

They pack customers in so close at **NATE'S DELI** at lunchtime that conversations sprout up everywhere. That's why this is such a great place to meet people—trust me. The Mediterranean food here is highly praised by regular customers, and the crowd is eclectic. Meet a pal for lunch at Nate's, and you might finish your meal with more friends than you started out with. Nate's is open Mon–Fri 10 a.m.–6 p.m. and Sat 10 a.m.–5 p.m.

Nate's Deli, 1923 W. 25th St., Cleveland, (216) 696-7529

Get on the team to work with children

Become a special events host at the **RAINBOW CHILDREN'S MUSEUM**, and you'll meet folks who love to work with children. The artists, fund-raisers, and program-mers who help plan events here get to let their inner child come out and play. Call the museum and ask about specific volunteer groups that are right for you. Open daily 10 a.m.–5 p.m.

Rainbow Children's Museum, 10730 Euclid Ave., Cleveland, (216) 791-7114

Play at the Kiddie Park

Besides being a great place to take a kid, the **MEMPHIS KIDDIE PARK** is a great place to meet other adults who have kids. This park offers miniature carnival rides appropriate for children under the age of seven, and is a spot where single parents, aunts, and uncles converge for an afternoon of inexpensive fun. While junior spends time on the ride, get to know his mom or dad. Memphis Kiddie Park is open weekend afternoons during the summer.

Memphis Kiddie Park, 10340 Memphis, Cleveland, (216) 941-5995

Walk the planks

Boardwalks have long been a place to stroll and be seen strolling, and **CLEVELAND'S BOARDWALK** on the West Bank of the Flats is no exception. People of all ages converge here on summer nights, especially Friday and Saturday, to people-watch with the hope of meeting someone new. Enjoy the friendly carnival atmosphere here—and smile; you never know who's going to walk by.

Nautica Boardwalk, Flats West Bank, Cleveland

Nightowl eggs

Nightowls descend on the **BIG EGG** just after the bars close on Friday and Saturday nights. This greasy spoon fills up with folks who are hungry for eggs and hash browns. The bright lights spotlight booze-filled patrons as the place buzzes with conversation. Grab a plate of anything and stick around through a second cup of coffee—you're sure to meet some interesting people. Open 24/7.

The Big Egg, 5107 Detroit Ave., Cleveland, (216) 961-8000

Put a "you" in PTA

Joining the **PTA** is a great way to meet people while sending a message to your kids that says, "I care." Each and every school sponsors a PTA of some sort, and the events that they put on are often terrific opportunities to **MEET NEIGHBORS** you never knew you had. Here's a tip: though the regular meetings tend (still!) to be mom-heavy, becoming a sports booster will get you mingling with parents of both sexes. If you are super busy, then volunteer for an easy assignment—but do volunteer.

365 ways to **meet people** in Cleveland

Have Big Fun

Regulars hang out at Big Fun to read the latest comic books or search for coveted, **KITSCHY COLLECTIBLES**. Entering this store crowded with joke items, novelties, whoopee cushions, and nostalgic toys gives you license to chat, and you could talk for hours while you paw through the merchandise. Make Big Fun a regular stop if you like what you see sitting on the shelves—and strolling the aisles. Sun–Wed noon–6 p.m., Thu noon–8 p.m., Fri–Sat 11 a.m.–9 p.m.

Big Fun, 1827 Coventry Rd., Cleveland Hts., (216) 371-4386

Say a prayer

Don't be surprised by the large crowd mingling at lunchtime services at **ST. JOHN'S CATHEDRAL** downtown. In fact, on Holy Days of Obligation, this is quite a singles hot spot. Noontime mass is designed to get you in and out with time to spare for lunch—so why not invite somebody along to get a quick bite with you after services? It's a wholesome place to meet someone.

St. John's Cathedral, 1007 Superior Ave., Cleveland, (216) 771-6666

Writers unite!

You don't have to be a published writer to come to Write On Cleveland, but you might meet some there. Each meeting features a speaker on such topics as **getting published**, making money as a freelancer, and doing research, followed by a Q and A session. Writers of all levels of ability and all genres are welcome. Bring some work to discuss, or just come to listen, learn, and meet other aspiring writers. The group meets every other Saturday from 1 p.m.–3 p.m. at the East Cleveland Public Library; no registration necessary, just show up.

Write On Cleveland, Ted Schwarz, (216) 249-3101
East Cleveland Public Library, downstairs auditorium, 14101 Euclid Ave., Cleveland, (216) 541-4128

Where Frisbee dogs take their humans

You've taught your dog all the new tricks, and now it's time for the two of you to show off. Put Fido in a car with his favorite Frisbee and head for the park. The **OHIO DOG AND DISC CLUB** sponsors events and get-togethers throughout the year where dogs and their owners meet to show off their tricks—and maybe learn some new ones. You don't need to sign up—just show up after calling to find out where and when the next meeting is.

Ohio Dog and Disc Club, (216) 662-9169

Where the intellectuals drink

EDISON'S PUB is like a Flats-in-miniature for intelligent people. Bands play here on what might be the smallest stage in Cleveland, darters try to hit a bull's-eye in the back room, and Tremont's trendies mill about by the bar. Strike up a conversation with almost anyone in this friendly pub and, if it goes well, suggest a walk out to the garden patio for some fresh air. Mon– Sat 5 p.m.–2:30 a.m., Sun 8 p.m.–2:30 a.m.

Edison's Pub, 2373 Professor St., Cleveland, (216) 522-0006

Visit the old world

The **OLD WORLD FESTIVAL** is among the largest street fairs in the nation, and why not? The Cleveland Slovenian community—which puts on the festival—is one of the most active ethnic groups in town. Enjoy Slovenian-style polka music and dancing while you sample food and drink from the Old World. If by some chance you get bored, announce that you're single to a group of grannies, and they'll have a series of candidates for you to meet in no time. The festival happens in August.

East 185th Street Old World Festival, East 185th St., Cleveland, (216) 261-3263

Commune on Coventry

Feeling out of touch with today's youth? Spend a weekend or summer evening strolling up and down **COVENTRY ROAD** in Cleveland Heights, and you'll see what they're up to. If you're young and own a skateboard, this is the place to show off your fashion sense and your angst. If you're not-so-young, commiserate with others about how different things were in the good old days, then resign yourself to a cup of coffee. The best time to stroll Coventry Road is Wed–Sat after 6 p.m.

Coventry Road, between Mayfield Rd. and Euclid Heights Blvd., Cleveland Hts.

Be folksy

For folk singing, folk dancing, or folklore, this is the place. The Kent State University **FOLK FESTIVAL** in December attracts fans from Northeast Ohio and beyond for a well-planned series of concerts, lectures, and other activities. Get to know the friendly attendees as you go from place to place hearing live music and storytelling. Call for the festival schedule.

Kent State University Folk Festival, Kent State University, Kent, (330) 672-3161

Meet the legal types

For a sure-fire way to meet a lawyer, attend the flurry of **JUDICIAL FUND-RAISERS** held every spring and fall. Dutiful legal professionals show up at as many of these events as possible to stay in favor with judges and talk law with their peers. It's a fun way to get to know the legal community socially, so contact the local Democratic and Republican headquarters to find out where and when the fundraisers are taking place this year.

Democratic Party Headquarters, (216) 621-9750
Republican Party Headquarters, (216) 621-5415

A different kind of football game—still a lively crowd

GAELIC FOOTBALL GAMES are just an excuse for a group of Irish and Irish-American guys to get together and have a party. Rivalries heat up on the field as players merge lacrosse, soccer, and football into one lively game. But once the score is final, the boys settle into a reverie, catching up on gossip and flirting with the girls. It's a fun way to spend the afternoon and a sure way to meet a strapping young lad. Call to find out when and where the games will be.

Gaelic Football Games/Irish Heritage Club 726 Avon-Belden Rd., Avon Lake, (440) 933-3413

Be at home on the range

If you're looking to improve your game and meet some new golf partners, get your time in at **THE RANGE GOLF PRACTICE**, where you can work on your stroke among friends. During the winter months, The Range features 40 heated stalls, and the courses are well lit at night, so you'll be able to see where your ball is going even if the sun's gone down. If you need a bit of coaching, call ahead to schedule time with an instructor. Mon–Fri 10 a.m.–9 p.m. and Sat–Sunday 9 a.m.–9 p.m.

The Range Golf Practice, 1325 Center Rd., at Rt. 83, Avon, (440) 937-9464

Pass the hot sauce

Encounter a sizable cross-section of Cleveland's Hispanic community on Friday or Saturday evenings at **TORTILLA FELIZ**. It's one of the most popular Mexican restaurants in Cleveland. Insiders dine here because they know the delicious food is prepared by students learning the restaurant biz. Fri–Sat 4:30 p.m.–11 p.m.

Tortilla Feliz, 2651 W. 14th St., Tremont, (216) 241-8385

Share the great outdoors

If your sense of adventure doesn't always match up with your budget, try the **INSTITUTE OF THE GREAT OUTDOORS** (IGO—get it?). It offers classes that bring novices face to face with a kayak or on a weekend camping trip. And IGO will see that you have the gear you need to try out sports, often at very low cost. IGO also caters to those who might be newcomers to a sport or activity, so you'll never feel like the class dummy if you don't know what you're doing. And the best part is being with other adults—sometimes entire families—who want a new experience, too. They offer classes quarterly; call to register and find out about times and dates.

Institute of the Great Outdoors, (216) 341-1704

Be a part of the show

Meet active folks from your neighborhood at **Community theaters**. Sign up for the next production, and even if you don't make the audition, you can still help out with props, stage management, ticket sales, costume design, concessions—you get the idea. Since each production takes months to put together, you'll spend lots of time with the cast and crew and will probably make some friends. It's fun, it's convenient, and if you do pass the audition you might even get discovered. Call your local community theater to find out how to get involved.

Go to the carnival

February brings a **BRAZILIAN CARNAVAL** to Cleveland to benefit the International Child Health Program of University Hospitals Health System. A costume is required, so don your best carnival outfit and dance to samba music, sample Brazilian food and local treats, and bid on silent auction items. The party attracts festive folks who like to let loose, and even if you come alone you'll be welcomed into the crowd. Visit www.carnavalcle.com for a schedule and to order tickets.

Carnival, www.carnavalcle.com

For athletes with a can-do attitude

You'll feel welcome at the many classes offered at the **YOU CAN DO IT SPORTS CENTER**. As the name says, it's all about attitude. This is an encouraging place to broaden your abilities. Loosen up at a yoga class or become a better biker in a stationary biking class. If you prefer to work out on your own, it's almost as easy to make friends in the gym. Call to find out about membership.

You Can Do It Sports and Life Centers, 15381 Royalton Rd., Strongsville, (440) 238-1390

Get in on a friendly game of pool

Jillian's is an **UPSCALE POOL HALL** designed with single people in mind. Patrons are encouraged to start up a friendly game of billiards with one another. More than a dozen pool tables here mean you won't have to wait long for a table, and soon you'll be chatting away with other stick players, getting advice on how to play or delivering a challenge for the next game. Open Mon–Thu 4 p.m.–1 a.m., Fri–Sat noon–2 a.m., and Sun 1 p.m–midnight.

Jillian's Billiard Club, 12459 Cedar Rd., Cleveland Hts., (216) 397-0900

Gather around the statue

Just before Indians games at Jacobs Field, a crowd gathers around the **BOB FELLER STATUE**. Some are there to meet a date, but many others are hooking up with friends. Before you go to the game, stop there to mingle with others in the crowd— talk baseball statistics or debate the merits of stadium mustard—then make plans to meet up for a seventh-inning stretch at the Gate A concession stand. America's favorite pastime is also Cleveland's best social glue.

Jacobs Field, 2401 Ontario St., Cleveland, (216) 420-4200

The best group run in the city

Cleveland DJ Billy Bass started the **BILLY BASS RUN TO HELP** with the humble expectation of raising a few bucks each week for locals in need. He never expected to raise more than $10,000 for the American Red Cross. At 9:00 a.m. every Saturday in the summer, an ever-growing group meets at Edgewater Park to run or walk for the cause, and they've created something of a community. Bass makes the event very social, encouraging newcomers to join, and the weekly event raises spirits as well as money. There is no formality to this run — nothing to sign up for — just show up with the desire to run or walk, and have a few bucks (at least $5 is encouraged) to donate.

Billy Bass Run to Help, Edgewater Park, 3600 John Nagy Blvd., Cleveland, (216) 881-8141

CLEVELAND FACT

More than 50 dance clubs make it possible to boogie at a
different spot every night of the week in Cleveland.

Be British for a day

Anglophiles unite! Though this event sounds hokey, it's a lot of fun. On **BRITISH CAR DAY** in August, British-car enthusiasts scoot around Shaker Square dressed up in turn-of-the-century costumes while stores on the square host teas and salons. You'll meet some of our town's more eclectic Anglophiles, see lovingly restored cars, and enjoy distinctly British entertainment. Call for the date.

British Car Day, Shaker Square, Shaker Hts., (216) 991-8700

What's brewing for beer buffs

Sure, it has become a tourist trap, but the beer garden at the **GREAT LAKES BREWING COMPANY** is still one of the best places for a Friday happy hour, especially if you're on the prowl. There always seem to be more men here than women, so girls, get your posse together and come on down. Sample the award-winning selection of beers while you eyeball a few draught fans. Enjoy the summer breeze in the brewery's outdoor beer garden or spend chilly winter nights in this cozy pub. Mon–Thu 11:30 a.m.–midnight, Fri–Sat 11:30 a.m.–1 a.m., and Sun 3 p.m.–9 p.m.

Great Lakes Brewing Company, 2516 Market Ave., Cleveland, (216) 771-4404

Stop by for open chess night

Live music, karaoke, and open chess night attract java junkies to **CYBER PETE'S INTERNET CAFÉ**. There's plenty of entertainment, offering lots of opportunity for interaction among the lively clientele. Call the café or check listings in your local paper to find out about upcoming events at Pete's, and show up to get connected with Cleveland's cyber community. Sun–Thu 6 p.m.–1 a.m., Fri 6 p.m.–2 a.m., Sat 9 p.m.–2 a.m.

Cyber Pete's Internet Café, 665 Broadway Ave., Bedford, (440) 439-5328

Meet a beach bum

Thousands of bare feet run across the beach at **EDGEWATER PARK** each summer, making this one of Cleveland's most popular destinations. Many are regulars—college kids with no summer jobs and tan-conscious adults who work the night shift. The social atmosphere begins around 11 a.m., when beach bums come out to optimize their time in the sun. Strike up a conversation by borrowing some tanning lotion or suggesting a walk to the concession stand, and take it from there.

Edgewater Park, 3600 John Nagy Blvd., Cleveland, (216) 881-8141

Where the diehard golf fans will be

It's the hottest ticket in town if you're into golf. Rub elbows with golf greats and golf lovers at the **NEC INVITATIONAL GOLF TOURNAMENT** at the fabulous Firestone Country Club in Akron. A number of charity events, including parties and other fund-raisers, surround this huge event, so call ahead to choose the parties you want to attend. Plan to spend a good deal of money, however, as these events are designed for the elite country club set. The tournament is held in August; call for a schedule and to order tickets.

NEC Invitational Golf Tournament, Firestone Country Club, Akron, (330) 644-2299

The next best thing to a trip to Asia

On Saturdays, **ASIA PLAZA** is brimming with shoppers who come for such imported items as red bean paste and soba noodles. Mingle at the import stores, or have lunch in the plaza, and you'll run into an eclectic group of people who are happy to help you find the right ingredients for miso soup. Become a Saturday morning regular, and the crowd here will start to look familiar—better yet, the shopkeepers will get to know you. Open daily 9 a.m.–7 p.m.

Asia Plaza, 2999 Payne Ave., Cleveland, (216) 241-3553

Talk with the animals

If you want to get close to animals, and people who like animals, volunteer to be an **ANIMAL HANDLER** at the Lake Erie Nature and Science Center. The Center staff will teach you everything you need to know to handle animals like snakes and raccoons, and to work with the public. Once you're comfortable in your role as live animal handler, they'll set you up with gigs all around the West Side, and you'll be a Science Center critter ambassador. Call to find out how.

Lake Erie Nature and Science Center, 28728 Wolf Rd., Bay Village, (440) 871-2900

Breathe new life

The Red Cross rewards volunteers with plenty of fun parties, get-togethers, and networking opportunities. And of course there are even bigger rewards. Teach a CPR class, and you might just save a life. Help stuff blankets into first aid kits, and a family might sleep comfortably tonight. Help draw blood this afternoon, and a child might be saved. You can do all these things and meet a great group of people by getting involved as a **RED CROSS VOLUNTEER**. Call to sign up.

American Red Cross Cleveland Chapter, 3747 Euclid Ave., Cleveland, (216) 431-3077

A multicultural crowd and Brazilian dance music

A trendy, multicultural crowd gathers at the **TOUCH SUPPER CLUB** on weekend nights. The resident DJ, Mazi Jahi, was working in the Warehouse District before it was ever cool, and has stayed on the cutting edge of cool ever since. Now part owner of this club, he spins records and oversees food preparation, while cool jazz and Brazilian rhythms send patrons to the basement for dancing. This crowd likes to dance and talk into the wee hours. Open for dinner Tue–Thu 5 p.m. –midnight, and Fri–Sat 5 p.m. –1 a.m.; it's open for dancing Thu–Sun 9 p.m.–2:30 a.m.

Touch Supper Club, 2710 Lorain Ave., Cleveland, (216) 631-5200

Share a snack at Sweetwater

People riding bikes, walking their dogs, and spinning on rollerblades all stop at **SWEETWATER** for a snack and to meet their fellow park-goers when they're at the Rocky River Reservation. Spending time here is a pleasure as you watch athletes of every variety mill about while you relax in the sun. Bask in the glow of a nice day, and remember to smile at everyone you meet. Sat–Sun 10 a.m.–8:30 p.m.

Sweetwater Landing at Rocky River Reservation, 1500 Scenic Park Dr., Lakewood, (216) 228-2233

A sledders' commune

If you think of sledding as soon as you see snowflakes, make your way to the South Chagrin Reservation Sledding Hill in the heart of the snowbelt. Here, an **IMPROMPTU GATHERING OF SLEDDERS** becomes a community as adults watch over the kids, and sledders compare the relative agility of various sledding mechanisms. Bring a cafeteria tray or a big plastic sheet—or be the big shot on the hill with a vintage rail sled—and spend the afternoon in a snowy paradise with other snow lovers.

South Chagrin Reservation Sledding Hill, at Sulfur Springs Dr. and Chagrin River Rd., Solon, (216) 351-6300

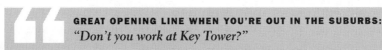

GREAT OPENING LINE WHEN YOU'RE OUT IN THE SUBURBS:
"Don't you work at Key Tower?"

A great club for the active set

The **CLEVELAND SPORT AND SOCIAL CLUB** tirelessly schedules events, organizes sports leagues, and puts on parties that bring Clevelanders—young and old—together for the love of sports and community. Get active on a planning committee, and soon you'll find your calendar filled. If you want less of a commitment but still want to join in the fun, call to find out which upcoming events appeal to you.

Cleveland Sport and Social Club, 1322 Old River Rd., Cleveland, (216) 696-3770

Outdoor concerts, but in an intimate setting

So much goes on at **CAIN PARK** during the summer that you're bound to run into someone you know or meet someone new at one of the concerts. Get a lawn seat ticket to a summer concert here—the prices are surprisingly low—and you'll be in the midst of a great group of people. Want to make yourself more popular? Bring a bottle of organic bug repellent. You'll be everybody's best friend as you pass around this valuable commodity. Call for a concert schedule.

Cain Park Summer Concerts, Superior & Lee Rds., Cleveland Hts., (216) 371-3000

Go marketing on Miles

The **MILES FARMERS MARKET** attracts a great group of people who love fresh food and share an interest in cooking. Fresh farm produce and meats bulge from the display tables. But if you shop here you'll be looking at more than just produce. On Saturday mornings, especially, the market is populated with healthy, perky shoppers eager to get the freshest produce before it's all gone. Stop down for a look at the goods. Mon–Fri 9 a.m.–8 p.m., and Sat–Sun 9 a.m.–6 p.m.

Miles Farmers Market, 28560 Miles Rd., Cleveland, (440) 248-5222

Super crowded, super fun

After 10 on weekend nights, the **LAVA LOUNGE** begins to heat up. Patrons enter with high expectations, wearing their best weekend outfits, and the DJ starts spinning the latest dance music. It's a crowded little place—but that's what makes it such a good time. The crowd is here to meet and greet, so order up some food (served until 1 a.m.) and mingle. Fri–Sat 9 p.m.–2:30 a.m.

Lava Lounge, 1307 Auburn Ave., Cleveland, (216) 589-9112

The insiders' jazz festival

The **Tri-C Jazz Festival** in April might be the most underrated annual festival in Cleveland. And that might be alright with Jazz fans—it keeps the riffraff out. But if you like jazz even just a little, you owe it to yourself to go. Diehards tend to stick around after a concert hoping for a surprise guest appearance by a beloved player, or a mix-and-mingle discussion of jazz that carries on into the late hours. If you're jazz-friendly, they'll be friendly to you. Call for the festival schedule.

Tri-C Jazz Festival, Cuyahoga Community College and at various locations, (216) 987-4444

Gather with gardeners

Get in touch with nature, and next to area garden fans by strolling through the **CLEVELAND BOTANICAL GARDEN**. Strike up a conversation with a stranger here, and you might not only find out how to get rid of slugs but also make a new friend. Better yet, take a class. They range from garden design to master gardening classes on how to grow difficult plants in Ohio soil. These courses let you meet others who enjoy getting their hands dirty and cultivating a green thumb. Stop in for a list of classes offered throughout the year, or call and they'll mail you a copy. Mon–Sat 9 a.m.–5 p.m., and Sun noon–5 p.m.

Cleveland Botanical Garden, 11030 East Blvd., Cleveland, (216) 721-1600

TIPS AND REMINDERS
Always carry business cards.

An old-fashioned bandstand concert

A stroll through the green in downtown Hudson is pleasant all by itself, but add an old-fashioned band concert to the picture, and you'll be transported to a more innocent time when ladies and gentlemen went out walking together. Call the city of Hudson to find out when concerts are taking place, then bring a few friends along with you to this **SOCIAL HUB**. If you live in the Hudson area, it's a great opportunity to meet and greet your neighbors, and if you live farther away, you'll enjoy mixing with a new group of people.

Hudson Bandstand Concerts, Hudson Park, at Main St. and St. Rte. 303, Hudson, (330) 673-5985

The largest beach holds the largest crowd

Meet sun worshippers at **MENTOR HEADLANDS**, where throngs of beach bums spend much of the summer. Because it is the largest sand beach along the Ohio portion of the Lake Erie shore, there's plenty of room for everyone, but it still gets mighty crowded here on weekends.

Mentor Headlands, at St. Rte. 2 and St. Rte. 44, Mentor, (216) 881-8141

Tailgate

For many Cleveland Browns fans, **TAILGATING** before games is a ritual. To join the party, get to the Cleveland Municipal Parking Lot two to four hours before a home game. Although there are many ways to introduce yourself to other tailgaters, the phrase "that smells good" serves as both a compliment and a request. If you're lucky, they'll give you a bratwurst and a bun, and let you socialize for a while.

Cleveland Municipal Parking Lot, Cleveland

Rock the town all summer long

Make a note in your daybook to reserve Wednesdays all summer long for **MUSIC** at the Rock and Roll Hall of Fame and Museum. The downtown crowd is drawn to the lake shore for these free weekly events that mix local talent with regional and national acts. Join in the fun and mingle with the who's who of Cleveland rockers in this festive atmosphere. The concerts run from 5:30 p.m.–7:30 p.m.

Free concerts at the Rock Hall, 1 Key Plaza, Cleveland, (888) 764-7625

Hit the Y after work

The refurbished **DOWNTOWN YMCA** draws a sizable after-work crowd of lively young to middle-aged professionals. If you really want to get to know your fellow flexers, join one of the many classes offered here. There are plenty of "gym flirts" to go around, and cliques begin to form leading to after workout jaunts for drinks or dinner. Call for membership information and class schedules. Mon–Fri 6 a.m.–9 p.m., Sat 8 a.m.–5 p.m., Sun 10 a.m.–3 p.m.

Downtown YMCA, 2200 Prospect Ave., Cleveland, (216) 344-7700

Get in on the ground floor of a budding theater group

There is a spirited group of people behind the recent success of the **NEAR WEST THEATRE**. And you can be a part of it. Because the group is still so young—they've only been active in the past few years—they need help with everything. Sign up to work on a marketing or outreach committee, and you'll be in with a group of professionals and volunteers who promote a theater that's worth getting excited about. Call to volunteer.

Near West Theater, 3610 Bridge Ave., Cleveland, (216) 651-2828

Meet college students and recent grads

Single college grads and students living in Northeast Ohio are welcome at events hosted by **THE COTERIE**. Group leaders make sure members feel welcome and get a chance to mingle with other college grads at the event. The Holiday Party is the Coterie's biggest event of the year, but tag along to any of their monthly events—if you attended college in Northeast Ohio, you're almost guaranteed to meet fellow alums here. Call to find out when the next event is happening, bring along a few of your college-graduate friends, and make a point of meeting two new people while you're there.

The Coterie, (330) 336-0421

TIPS AND REMINDERS

Make friends with socially active people. If you're at all shy, hang out with outgoing people—often. They might throw you into uncomfortable situations, but once you get the hang of it, you'll be grateful for the many people you meet.

Downtown's busiest food court

You won't meet anyone if you have lunch at your desk, so make your way over to the **food court**. Downtown's favorite meeting place is the food court at Tower City. Because the food court is such a popular destination, tables fill up quickly, and often if you're lunching on your own you'll have to share a table with a stranger. Pick out one who seems interesting, look just a tad disheveled, and ask, "Can I sit here?" Soon, you could be chatting about common interests over fries and a burger. Toss a penny in the fountain on your way out for luck. You never know what might happen.

Tower City food court, 1500 West 3rd., Cleveland, (216) 736-7646

Go to Cleveland's own film festival

Even moderate movie fans should spend a few days at the **CLEVELAND INTERNA-TIONAL FILM FESTIVAL**. Serious film buffs should plan their calendar around it. For 10 days each March, this showcase of world-class films brings more than 30,000 people downtown, and most of them want to talk about one thing: films. Many parties and activities surround the film schedule. Call for the schedule.

Cleveland Film Festival, Tower City Center, Cleveland, (call Cleveland Film Society for information (216) 623-3456)

Share a cause

If you want to get involved in politics on the grassroots level, look to **COMMON CAUSE**. With dogged dedication, the activists of Common Cause keep watch over the political system on a local level. They need your help with everything—from making sure workers' rights are upheld to getting the word out about legislative issues that affect us all. Because of the long hours involved, and the passions of the dedicated people who volunteer for campaigns, this is one of the best bonding experiences you can have. Call to volunteer.

Common Cause, (216) 961-3031

See at least one game from the dawg pound

It looks nutty on TV, but the **DAWG POUND** at Cleveland Browns Stadium is among the friendliest places in town (as long as you're not a Steelers fan). The diehards who watch the game here watch *every* game here, so get season tickets or try to pick up a single from a scalper if you want to find pals in the pound.

Cleveland Browns Stadium, (440) 891-5050

Join a golf league

"Golf leagues always want new members," says John Tidyman, author of *The Cleveland Golfer's Bible*. "The **CLEVELAND INDUSTRIAL GOLF LEAGUE** is the grandaddy of them all [it's more than 60 years old]. Join and all of a sudden you have a primo tee-time at courses all over Cleveland every Saturday morning." Join as an individual and you'll get "drafted" by a team. League members have handicaps as high as 30, so you don't have to be a hotshot. You don't have to play every week, but it does require some commitment. Sorry ladies, this league is guys-only (but check out the next entry!). Also, ask at your local golf course; most host a couple of leagues.

Cleveland Industrial Golf League, (440) 234-4321, www.cigl.org

Golf with executive women

Since 1992, the Executive Women's Golf League has been helping women take up the game of golf for fun, friendship, and networking. Get on the league (membership is $100 for the season) and get out on the links with **LOCAL WOMEN GOLFERS**. Cleveland members play at Pine Hills, Pine Ridge, The Links, and Highland. In addition to regular league play, the EWG league features monthly events for getting to know your fellow golfers outside of the game. Call about membership.

Executive Women's Golf League, Cleveland Chapter, P.O. Box 31704, Independence, (216) 999-9664

A little place with a big lunch crowd

Want to hang with an intellectual, health-conscious set? Grab lunch at **TEAHOUSE NOODLES**, a little restaurant that draws a big crowd for lunch. Order a cooked-to-order plate and take a seat in the crowded dining room. People sit so close together here that they often strike up conversations with strangers. Become a regular and see who you bump into at lunch. Mon–Fri 11 a.m.–2 p.m.

Teahouse Noodles, 1900 E. 6th St., Cleveland, (216) 623-9131

An art show for the very social

Lakewood is one of Cleveland's most congested and busy suburbs, and is also among the most socially vibrant communities in the area—so the odds are in your favor for meeting someone here, especially at the **LAKEWOOD ARTS FESTIVAL** held every August. The crowd here is young and old, cultured and not so cultured, but when they get together there is no pretense—just art, entertainment, and plenty of mingling. Call for a festival schedule.

Lakewood Arts Festival, Detroit Ave. and Warren Rd., Lakewood, (216) 529-6651

Cleveland's quirkiest rock 'n' roll

The energy level at the spunky **BEACHLAND BALLROOM** is usually high. Owners Cindy Barber and Mark Lette have created a venue that allows them to share their love of quirky rock and roll with all of Cleveland. The acts are carefully booked to ensure a healthy mix of kitsch, intelligence, and fun. Regulars here don't even check the listings anymore—they know that any night at the Beachland will be lively. Daily 8 p.m.–2:30 a.m.

Beachland Ballroom, 15711 Waterloo Rd., Cleveland, (216) 383-1124

DANCE Cleveland, Dance

If you like attending dance performances, why not get more involved with the dance community in Cleveland? Creative workshops, master classes, and a season filled with cutting-edge performances make **DANCE CLEVELAND** an inspiring group to be a part of. Help support them by volunteering time at the office, or simply by subscribing to their performance series. Once you've been to a performance or two, you'll start getting to know the regulars. Call to volunteer.

DANCE Cleveland, 1148 Euclid Ave., # 311, Cleveland, (216) 861-2213

Shop where the chefs shop

There's a secret to meeting people at the **WEST SIDE MARKET**. You have to be sneaky. If someone catches your eye, follow him or her around until they are about to buy something, then ask, "How do you cook that?" Most of the patrons who shop here like to cook; if you play your cards right, you might be cooking for two in short order. Mon and Wed 7 a.m.–4 p.m., and Fri–Sat 7 a.m.–6 p.m.

West Side Market, 2501 1979 W. 25th St., Cleveland, (216) 664-3386

Join the Opera League

Dress-up parties, opportunities to meet some of the biggest opera stars in the world, and an elegant annual gala make the **CLEVELAND OPERA LEAGUE** one of the most prestigious local organizations you can join. If you like opera, but don't want to don the swishy formals then just attend the league's lectures and programs, where you can get all the intellectual benefits without the fancy outfits. Call for membership information.

Cleveland Opera League, 1422 Euclid Ave, Cleveland, (216) 575-0903

The closest thing to a crowded New York City street

Up and down the street you go, and if you don't like the crowd at one **WEST 6TH STREET** location, just amble on to the next. Almost every demographic is represented on this street, which bustles with taxis, limousines, and foot traffic throughout the weekend. There's a boulevard atmosphere as groups yell to each other, making plans or trying to get together. Enjoy the buzz of people and activity as you head toward new encounters. Most of the bars are open daily 8 p.m.–2:30 a.m.

Warehouse District, W. 6th and 9th Sts., from Lakeside to Superior, Cleveland

Marriages begin here

Those who work in the Playhouse Square district know that the food court at the Halle Building has taken on a reputation as a place where MARRIAGES begin. Set on the lower level, it's really just an accumulation of fast-food lines, but the young crowd seems more talkative during the lunch hour. Enter this fast-food Mecca at lunchtime and find out how much fun a food court can be.

Halle Building Food Court, 1288 Euclid Ave., Cleveland, (216) 696-7701

Network with networkers

Involved in the information technology industry? Then you should be at the Northeast Ohio **Software Association's** next monthly meeting. This is an active group of software professionals and young techies, and its meetings, held in the tasting room at the Great Lakes Brewing Company, are a lot of fun. Membership has benefits: networking, professional development (how about signing up for a workshop called "Entreprenerd Bootcamp"?), and a listing in the association's directory. Nonmembers are welcome to attend the monthly meetings. Call NEOSA to find out where and when the next meeting will be.

Northeast Ohio Software Association, 50 Public Square # 200, Cleveland, (216) 592-2257

Where nature lovers love to go

The Nature Center at Shaker Lakes hosts classes and programs throughout the year that range from beginning hiking to advanced environmental issues that impact the SHAKER LAKES. This place is always brimming with activity, so stop by to find out more about classes that are offered, programs you can participate in, and group walks and hikes around this lovely area.

Nature Center at Shaker Lakes, 2600 S. Park Blvd., Shaker Hts., (216) 321-5935

The most visible seat in town

Grab a table inside **PRESTI'S**, a sleekly styled patisserie, or—during the summer months—grab a sidewalk seat, which gives you a close-up view of the people strolling up and down Mayfield Road in Little Italy. Patrons standing at the pastry case often exclaim to perfect strangers, "Look at that!" as they point to a creative confection, and regulars are more than happy to help steer newcomers to the right treat. Open Sun–Thu 6 a.m.–7 p.m., and Fri–Sat 6 a.m.–10 p.m.

Presti's Bakery, 12101 Mayfield Rd., Cleveland, (216) 421-3060

Just like spring break all over again

You have to enjoy partying, late nights, and loud music to enjoy **PUT-IN-BAY**. But if triple threat appeals to you, there's no better place than this party island to meet new people on a summer weekend. That's what almost everybody on the island is there to do. Stay at a hotel, or look in the *Plain Dealer* for the many cabin and condo rentals that are available, and plan to spend at least one night on the island. Call the Put-in-Bay info line for lodging and entertainment information.

Put-in-Bay Chamber of Commerce info line, (419) 285-2832

Exchange culture

If you enjoy being involved with kids, then A Cultural Exchange is a fantastic organization to get involved with. This Northeast Ohio not-for-profit is dedicated to helping children learn to **READ AND ENJOY BOOKS**. Volunteers at the bookstore meet the public while advancing the cause, and volunteers for the book drives get out in the community to collect donations. While you're collecting books for kids, maybe you'll book a date as well. Call to volunteer.

A Cultural Exchange, 12621 Larchmere Blvd., Cleveland, (216) 229-8300

Play it cool with the beautiful people

Trend-setters come here to impress, so wear your club clothes and play it cool if you decide to go. **WISH** is a dance club with attitude in the Warehouse District. It's good to bring a friend along; people here are on the make, but not too many come stag. Thu–Sat 7 p.m.–2:30 a.m.

Wish, 621 Johnson Ave., Cleveland, (216) 902-9474

Theater by the seat-of-your-pants

Sign up for a volunteer assignment at the **BEREA SUMMER THEATER**—acting, teaching, building sets—and you'll meet a community of dedicated theater types who put on a slew of shows in a short season. It's a no-business-like-show-business, seat-of-your-pants experience that will forge lasting relationships extending well into the winter months. Call to volunteer.

Berea Summer Theater, 95 E. Bagley Rd., Berea, (440) 826-2240

Train to be a nature guide

Volunteer to lead walks through the **ARBORETUM** and you'll meet a new group of people to meet every time. People who come here are already interested in nature; they just need a guide. Trained staff at the arboretum will help familiarize you with the grounds and the tours, and won't send you off with a group until you're ready. If you don't want to lead hikes, help at the front desk—you'll still be in this lovely setting, meeting and greeting an appreciative crowd all day. Call to sign up.

Holden Arboretum, 9500 Sperry Rd., Kirtland, (440) 946-4400

A night out with movie stars

For an evening of glitz and glamour, attend the annual **OSCAR NIGHT PARTY** sponsored by the AIDS Task Force. The organizers go all out to make the party almost more interesting than the actual awards show. Dress to the nines and walk up to the party on a red carpet. Joan Crawford—or someone just like her—will greet you at the door. Everyone here wants to share their opinions about the movies, so this party is full of conversation. The party begins at 7 on Oscar night; call for ticket information.

AIDS Task Force, (call Cleveland Health Museum (216) 231-5010)

Support for single parents

Find a supportive environment for single parents at **PARENTS WITHOUT PARTNERS**. You are welcome to attend everything from support group meetings to parties where parents and children gather to play and blow off steam. Many events are structured so that children can come along, but still more are adults only, allowing parents time to relax and socialize together. Call to find out the next meeting time and place.

Parents Without Partners, (330) 258-1001

You don't have to be a doctor . . .

If you're a healthcare professional, consider becoming an active member at the **HEALTH MUSEUM** of Cleveland. Programs here are geared toward kids—but the adults are crucial to the process. By volunteering, you will work with other health-care professionals to put on seminars like Junior Medical Camp, where children learn the basics about the field of medicine from you. Volunteers for such programs are needed to teach the classes or to assist with getting the kids from one session to another. You don't have to have an advanced degree to be a part of these learning programs, but you'll likely meet plenty of people who do. Contact the museum to find out how you can help.

Health Museum, 8911 Euclid Ave., Cleveland, (216) 231-5010

CLEVELAND FACT

Cleveland has more than 100 community centers and community theater groups that are great places to meet the people in your neighborhood.

Join the crew

An energized group of theater enthusiasts makes up the **CLEVELAND PLAYHOUSE CREW**. They throw parties, attend play openings together, and meet regularly to talk theater. Join up with this group, and you'll have an inside track to some of this town's best thespian efforts while you meet the young professionals and creative types who are attracted to this group. Call to volunteer.

Cleveland Playhouse Crew, 8501 Carnegie Ave., Cleveland, (216) 795-1111

Cruise

Cruiser-style motorcycle owners meet to cruise the streets of Cleveland and travel to the annual rally somewhere in America each year. Find someone to ride with — and get parts from — by joining the **THE CRUISER CLUB OF CLEVELAND**, and you'll never have to cruise the streets alone again. Of course, you should own a cruiser-style motorcycle to join. If you do, call the group to find out when and where they'll be meeting next.

Cruiser Club, USA Cleveland Chapter, (440) 461-5978

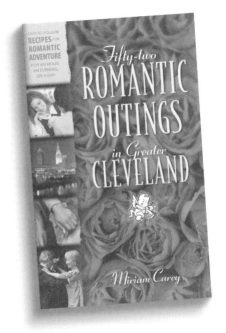